EXPLOSIVE
CONNECTIONS

Building Business Through
Strategic Relationships

JANELLE KENNEDY

ISBN: 978-1-968061-79-1

Table of Contents

Foreword

When Janelle first told me she was writing a book on networking, I wasn't surprised. No one embodies the art of authentic connection like she does. But here's the thing – Janelle's approach to networking isn't what you might expect. It's not transactional. It's not about collecting business cards or making quick introductions or looking past someone in conversation to see who you can talk to next.

So many of us approach networking with a "what's in it for me?" mindset. Not Janelle. She builds relationships that last because she genuinely cares. She listens, she sees people, and she helps them recognize their own potential. And she does it effortlessly.

I watched her do this just recently. A mutual friend of ours was at a crossroads in her career, unsure of what she was going to do next. Through a few thoughtful conversations, Janelle helped her gain clarity about her unique gifts. Within weeks, Janelle connected her with an opportunity that changed the trajectory of her career in a way that leaves our friend fulfilled and excited about the future.

That's the Janelle magic. It's second nature for her. She doesn't network to get ahead; she networks to lift others up. I know this firsthand. What started as a simple work connection between us has grown into a deep friendship and partnership, built on mutual respect and support.

Janelle's philosophy isn't just about growing your network – it's about growing your community, your confidence, and your connection to the people around you. In a world where networking often feels forced and self-serving, Building Business Relationships is Fundamental, not Optional is a breath of fresh air. It's not just a book, it's an invitation to do things differently... to build relationships that are real, meaningful, and built to last.

If you've ever felt disconnected, uncertain, or like networking just isn't "your thing," this book will change the way you see it. Let Janelle show you how your connections can be authentic, fulfilling, and yes – even fun.

Nina Radetich
Certified EOS Implementer® at EOS Worldwide

Meet the Author: Janelle

ENERGY FREQUENCY

I thrive on social connections and building relationships, finding it completely natural to make new friends and get along with people from all walks of life. While I can power through them when necessary, detailed tasks like poring over spreadsheets or instruction manuals tend to drain my energy rather than energize me.

This natural inclination toward human connection has been my greatest professional asset throughout my career. Whether I'm walking into a room full of strangers at a networking event or facilitating introductions between two professionals who could benefit from knowing each other, I feel energized by the possibilities that emerge from authentic interaction. The spark of excitement I feel when I see potential synergies between people or businesses isn't just professional enthusiasm—it's what fuels my daily work and drives my passion for helping others succeed.

What truly lights me up is witnessing the moment when a connection I've facilitated blossoms into something meaningful—a partnership, a friendship, a business opportunity that transforms someone's trajectory. These moments remind me why relationship-building isn't just what I do professionally; it's who I am at my core. My energy naturally flows toward creating spaces where authentic connections can flourish, and I've built my entire business around this fundamental truth about myself.

SUPERPOWERS

My greatest strength lies in my natural ability to connect with and understand people. I possess an innate talent for bringing individuals together and fostering meaningful relationships. This is complemented by my strategic mindset, which allows me to recognize patterns in data and information. I have a keen eye for identifying and maximizing potential, both in myself and others, coupled with a genuine passion for helping people grow and develop. My infectious energy and enthusiasm light up any room I enter, and I maintain an unwavering positivity that influences those around me. Perhaps most notably, I possess an endless reservoir of energy that drives me to turn ideas into action, consistently pushing projects forward and getting things done.

What sets me apart is my ability to see connections and opportunities that others often miss. I can quickly assess a room and identify who should meet whom, or listen to someone describe their business challenges and immediately envision solutions or resources that could help. This intuitive understanding of how different pieces fit together—whether it's people, businesses, or ideas—allows me to serve as a catalyst for transformation in both individual lives and entire professional communities. My superpower isn't just making connections; it's seeing the bigger picture of how those connections can create exponential value for everyone involved.

MY JOURNEY

The seeds of entrepreneurship were planted early in my life. At just eight years old, while other young girls were playing with dolls, I was already displaying the business acumen that would define my career. As a true unicorn – actually born and raised in Las Vegas, my path has been as unique as my hometown. From setting up mock restaurants and grocery stores to creating my own payment systems complete with handwritten checks, my entrepreneurial spirit was unmistakable. I would coordinate with the kids in the neighborhood to direct puppet shows, organizing performances and managing the entire production. When my mother became an Avon representative as a stay-at-home mom, at 8 years old I eagerly took the reins, managing orders and deliveries with remarkable efficiency. Despite coming from a blue-collar family of construction workers in 1970s Las Vegas, I naturally gravitated toward business and white-collar pursuits, later pursuing secretarial and business studies to build a strong foundation for my future career.

Not everyone can wear both the marketing and sales hats—and truly wear them well. My professional journey is a testament to the power of embracing both creativity and strategic execution. Where many professionals find themselves siloed into either marketing ideation or sales implementation, I've discovered the extraordinary potential that emerges when these disciplines are masterfully integrated.

My marketing ability is inherently visionary—I see possibilities where others see limitations. It's an intuitive process of understanding market dynamics, crafting compelling narratives, and identifying unique value propositions. This isn't just about creating attractive messaging; it's about developing a holistic view of how a business can truly connect with its audience.

Sales, on the other hand, is my honed skill—a craft I've refined through decades of practical experience. From my early days coordinating pyrotechnics for legendary acts like Michael Jackson, Guns N' Roses, and Metallica to my subsequent roles in real estate and business development, I've transformed sales from a transactional process to an art of genuine connection.

My professional odyssey began dramatically in the early 1990s as a Pyrotechnic Coordinator, managing logistics for global entertainment acts. This experience was my first masterclass in high-pressure precision—understanding that success requires both creative vision and meticulous execution. Managing complex productions taught me that true professional excellence lies in bridging imagination with implementation.

The late 1990s saw me transition into real estate, where I expanded my talents as an Account Executive, diving deep into Home Warranty and Title/Escrow industries. Far more than a traditional service provider, I positioned myself as a strategic partner to realtors. My approach went well beyond transactional interactions—I became a trusted advisor, helping real estate professionals identify and penetrate target markets with precision and creativity.

I developed comprehensive strategies that empowered realtors to expand their business reach. This meant not just offering services but providing actionable marketing intelligence. My unique value proposition was transforming standard industry services into strategic business growth tools.

This holistic approach—combining deep market understanding, creative marketing strategies, and precise sales execution—became my signature method. I wasn't just selling a service; I was offering a pathway to business growth and success.

What sets me apart is the seamless integration of these skills. Marketing provides the vision, the story, the compelling "why" behind a business. Sales transforms that vision into tangible results, building relationships and driving growth. Where others see these as separate disciplines, I see them as two sides of the same coin—each amplifying the other's potential.

My childhood entrepreneurial spirit, nurtured through years of professional experience, ultimately led to founding Jayde Consulting in 2022. As CEO and Business Development Consultant, I now help local businesses unlock their full potential by applying this integrated approach. Whether working with established companies or aspiring entrepreneurs, I bring a holistic perspective that combines creative marketing vision with precision sales execution.

In a world of specialization, I've built a career on versatility. Marketing and sales aren't just job functions for me—they're interconnected art forms that, when practiced with passion and insight, can transform businesses and create meaningful impact.

INTRODUCTION

The Power of Connection

It all started with pyrotechnics - a world where relationships were the difference between success and failure. In those high-stakes productions, success hinged on connections with tour managers, production teams, and entertainment companies. Each conversation was a potential pathway to the next opportunity, and I quickly learned that building a reputation for reliability meant nurturing every professional relationship.

The most rewarding moments weren't just the spectacular displays that lit up stadiums - they were when months of relationship-building culminated in extraordinary collaborations that transformed vision into reality.

Fast forward to 2016, when another unexpected connection would reshape my professional trajectory. Gary Laney discovered my profile on LinkedIn and invited me to host a networking chapter. As a title/escrow representative focused exclusively on real estate agents and lenders, this opportunity would push me far beyond my comfortable niche. Despite my hesitation, I took that leap of faith - a decision that would completely transform my professional path.

Immersing myself in this new community of diverse business owners and professionals was transformative. The depth of relationships, breadth of perspectives, and richness of connections left me hungry for more. This wasn't just networking for immediate business opportunities; it was about creating a community of support, learning, and mutual growth.

This experience catalyzed what would become my passionate approach to networking. It taught me that limiting ourselves to immediate industry connections means missing out on countless opportunities for growth and meaningful relationship building. The most valuable connections often come from the most unexpected places.

From pyrotechnic productions to professional networking, one truth has remained constant: relationships are the explosive force that can illuminate entire professional landscapes.

As I dove deeper into the art of networking, hosting groups and serving as chapter president for women's organizations, I witnessed hundreds of connections bloom into collaborations, friendships, and game-changing opportunities. I discovered that networking isn't just a business skill; it's the invisible architecture of success.

The magic lies in the intricate web of genuine relationships formed when professionals come together with open minds and authentic intentions. These connections create ripples extending far beyond initial interactions, laying the groundwork for transformative professional relationships.

But the most powerful connections often form when you're not trying to force them. They happen when you show up consistently, listen intently, and give generously without immediate expectation of return. The most successful networkers aren't those with the biggest contact lists; they're the ones who have mastered being genuinely interested and helpful.

Effective networking is about emotional intelligence, authenticity, and creating meaningful connections in a world that often prioritizes quantity over quality. It's understanding that every person carries a universe of experiences and possibilities that could align with your path in unpredictable ways.

Through building my business on the power of networking, I've seen that the most successful professionals cultivate relationships like master gardeners. They plant seeds of connection, nurture them with consistent attention, and patiently watch their network grow into a flourishing ecosystem of opportunities, support, and mutual growth.

This book is a roadmap to understanding and harnessing the invisible forces connecting people and possibilities. Through these pages, I'll share strategies, techniques, and real stories of transformation that prove the enduring power of the human element in business.

Why Relationships Matter in Personal and Professional Success

In our hyperconnected world, it's easy to mistake digital connections for real relationships. But genuine human connections remain the bedrock of both personal fulfillment and professional achievement.

Consider the last professional crisis you faced. Did you post on LinkedIn for answers or reach out to a trusted colleague you've built a real relationship with over time? In moments of true need, we turn to people we've connected with meaningfully, not superficial social media contacts.

Science reveals what successful networkers have long known intuitively: human connections reshape our brain chemistry. Meaningful social interactions release oxytocin, the "trust hormone," helping us form bonds and build trust in ways that online interactions simply can't replicate.

Moreover, professional relationships operate on a "compound interest principle." Just as money grows exponentially through compound interest, relationships grow in value through accumulated trust, shared experiences, and mutual support. A single strong relationship connects you not just to one person, but to their entire network, knowledge base, opportunities, and resources. This explains why some professionals seem consistently "lucky" - they're benefiting from years of relationship compound interest.

Successful professionals treat relationship-building as a fundamental part of their identity. They show up consistently, remember details, follow up, and add value proactively. These are habits that create a foundation for lasting success.

Every meaningful professional relationship also serves as a mirror for personal growth, offering new perspectives and helping refine our skills and emotional intelligence. For women in business especially, strong relationships can help navigate unique challenges and break through traditional barriers.

As you read on, you'll discover that the most valuable professional relationships come not from rigid networking formulas, but from genuine curiosity, authenticity, and willingness to invest without immediate expectations. Because ultimately, your success - professional and personal - is determined by the depth and quality of the relationships you build.

In the coming chapters, we'll explore the essential building blocks of strong connections and how to transform superficial networking into deep, meaningful relationships. Let's begin this journey together.

CHAPTER I

Beyond the Business Card Shuffle: Making Connections That Actually Stick

The Connection Workshop: Crafting Real Relationships

Imagine this: You've just taken over as the decor chair for a non-profit gala, stepping into the role previously held by Monica, a seasoned volunteer. As you connect with Monica to ensure a smooth transition, you feel an instant rapport - a sense that this handover of responsibilities is the beginning of something more meaningful than a mere volunteer role swap.

Fast forward several years, and that initial connection has blossomed into a vibrant partnership. You and Monica have collaborated on numerous events, women's panels, workshops, and networking engagements. Her company, Nevada Business Advisors, helps entrepreneurs navigate every aspect of starting and growing a successful venture. Together, you've become a dynamic duo, dedicated to bringing value to your local business community.

This, my friends, is the essence of crafting real relationships. It's not about the quantity of business cards collected or the perfection of your elevator pitch. It's about those genuine moments of connection, where shared passions and complementary strengths align to create something greater than the sum of its parts.

When you approach networking with an open heart, a curious mind, and a willingness to give generously of your time and expertise, you lay the foundation for relationships that transcend transactional interactions. You create the space for serendipity to work its magic, bringing people into your life who not only support your professional growth but also enrich your personal journey.

This is the ideal networking interaction - one that leaves both parties feeling energized, inspired, and genuinely connected. It's the kind of interaction that plants the seeds of long-term collaboration, mutual support, and shared success.

As you'll discover throughout this chapter, crafting real relationships requires a shift in mindset and approach. It means moving beyond the superficiality of the business card shuffle and instead focusing on creating genuine value for others. It means being present, curious, and authentic in every interaction. And it means nurturing connections with care and consistency over time.

My own journey with Monica is a testament to the power of this approach. What began as a transition of volunteer roles has grown into one of my longest-standing and most fruitful professional partnerships. Through our collaboration, we've not only elevated our own businesses but have also had the privilege of supporting countless other entrepreneurs along the way.

So as we dive into the art and science of making connections that stick, I invite you to think back to your own "Monica moment" - a time when a genuine connection opened up new possibilities and pathways in your professional journey. Hold onto that feeling of excitement, potential, and authentic connection. Because that's the feeling we're striving to create with every interaction as we master the craft of relationship building.

Just as no architect would construct a skyscraper without a proper foundation, no lasting professional relationship can be built without careful groundwork. Understanding the architecture of relationships is crucial to creating connections that stand the test of time and bear the weight of shared goals and challenges.

Think of relationship building as constructing a custom home. Before the first stone is laid, an architect spends considerable time understanding the terrain, studying the soil composition, and planning for both current needs and future expansion. They assess the ground's stability, drainage, and potential for supporting a structure, ensuring a solid, reliable foundation.

Similarly, crafting strong professional relationships requires careful consideration of your landscape, goals, and long-term vision. Just as an architect surveys the land, you must take time to understand the environment and people you're hoping to build connections with. This involves researching industry trends, assessing your own networking objectives, and evaluating opportunities that align with your aims.

By "studying the soil composition" in this way, you lay the groundwork for building genuine, mutually beneficial relationships that have the best chance of thriving over time. You ensure you're planting your networking seeds in the most fertile ground and creating a strong base for meaningful connection.

The foundation phase of relationship building isn't glamorous. There are no immediate wins, no quick victories to celebrate. Many skip this methodical work in their eagerness to "network," but this preliminary phase determines whether your professional relationships will withstand the tests of time and opportunity.

Let's get started on mastering the art of laying strong foundations. In the next section, we'll explore the key components of a solid relational groundwork and how to implement them in your own networking practice.

Get ready to roll up your sleeves and dive into exploring these three pillars of foundation work: Self-Assessment and Goal Clarity, Environmental

Analysis, and Resource Allocation. By focusing on these areas, you'll start building connections that will support your professional growth for years to come.

The rewards of this foundational work will reveal themselves in the enduring relationships you cultivate and the opportunities that emerge from a network built on authentic understanding and shared purpose. So let's get started laying the groundwork for a strong, purposeful network that will help you achieve your goals and make a meaningful impact in your professional journey.

3

Pillars of Foundation Work

SELF-ASSESSMENT AND GOAL CLARITY	ENVIRONMENTAL ANALYSIS	RESOURCE ALLOCATION
• Before you can build meaningful connections, you must understand what you're building toward • Define your professional objectives with specificity • Identify the gaps in your current network • Recognize your own relationship-building strengths and weaknesses	• Study your professional ecosystem • Understand where valuable connections naturally gather • Identify the power nodes in your industry • Map the relationship landscape	• Determine how much time you can realistically invest • Assess your relationship-building energy capacity • Plan for consistent, sustainable engagement • Set realistic expectations for growth

The art of selective connection is one of the most common mistakes I've observed in my years of leading professional groups is the tendency to treat all networking opportunities as equal. They are not! Just as a builder carefully selects materials that meet specific structural requirements, you must be selective about where and with whom you invest your relationship-building energy.

Finding the Right Fit: Networking Groups and Professional Organizations

Not all networking groups will serve your goals, and that's okay. I learned this lesson the hard way in my early days of networking. I was a member of four different professional organizations, attending every event I could squeeze into my calendar. I was busy, exhausted, and not seeing the results I wanted. It wasn't until I stepped back and evaluated each group against my specific needs that I began to see real progress. I became very intentional about where I was putting my energy.

Consider these factors when evaluating networking opportunities:

1. Alignment with Goals

- Does the group serve your target industry or profession?
- Are the members at a professional level where meaningful exchange is possible?
- Does the group's culture match your relationship-building style?

2. Quality of Interactions

- Does the group facilitate deep connections or just superficial exchanges?
- Are there opportunities for ongoing engagement beyond events?
- How does the group structure support relationship building?

3. Return on Investment

- How much time and energy does meaningful participation require?
- What is the quality of connections you're making?
- Are you seeing progress toward your professional goals?

The Strategic Conversation: Building Blocks of Strong Relationships

Once you've identified promising networking environments, the real foundation work begins through strategic conversations. These aren't your typical small talk network; they're purposeful exchanges designed to test compatibility and explore potential for mutual value.

Strategic conversations unfold through several essential phases, each building upon the other to create meaningful professional relationships. The **discovery phase** sets the foundation, where thoughtful questioning reveals what I call a person's "professional DNA." This goes beyond surface-level inquiries about their role or company—it's about understanding their vision, challenges, and aspirations. Through careful listening during this phase, we can identify areas of mutual interest and opportunity, while recognizing shared values and complementary goals that might form the basis for future collaboration.

As the conversation progresses, it naturally flows into **value exchange**. This crucial phase isn't about immediate reciprocity; rather, it's about identifying and creating opportunities to contribute meaningfully before expecting anything in return. By sharing relevant insights and resources that align with their needs and challenges, we demonstrate our potential value as a connection. These moments of meaningful assistance often become the memorable touchpoints that distinguish our interaction from countless other networking conversations.

The final, and often overlooked, element is the **follow-up framework.** This is where most networking efforts fall short, but it's actually where the real relationship-building begins. It's essential to develop a systematic approach to maintaining promising connections—not through generic "checking in" messages, but through thoughtful, specific next steps that create opportunities for deeper engagement. This might involve sharing a relevant article, making a strategic introduction, or planning a focused follow-up conversation around a specific topic or opportunity.

What transforms a good strategic conversation into an exceptional one is the element of authentic curiosity combined with professional vulnerability. The most powerful connections emerge when both parties are willing to share not just their successes, but their genuine challenges and areas where they're seeking growth. This creates what I call "connection chemistry"— that moment when two professionals realize they can genuinely help each other in unexpected ways. It's in these moments of mutual openness that surface-level networking transforms into the foundation for lasting professional partnerships that can weather industry changes, career transitions, and evolving business needs.

The Trial and Error Process

Building strong foundations requires patience and a willingness to learn from mistakes. Not every conversation will lead to a lasting connection. Not every group will prove valuable. Not every investment of time will yield returns. This isn't failure, it's the necessary refinement process that leads to stronger, more valuable relationships.

The journey of relationship building requires consistent reflection and adaptation to truly master its nuances. Regular assessment is crucial to this learning process—I make it a point to review my relationship-building activities quarterly, taking time to evaluate the quality of connections I'm making and honestly assess which approaches are yielding the best results. This regular review allows me to identify patterns and make necessary adjustments before too much time passes.

Through this ongoing evaluation, I've developed refinement strategies that help me continuously improve my networking effectiveness. I maintain detailed notes about what works and what doesn't, paying special attention to identifying patterns in my most successful connections. This documentation becomes invaluable as I modify my approach based on real feedback and tangible results. Understanding these patterns has helped me refine my networking strategy and avoid repeating less effective approaches.

The key to long-term networking success lies in commitment to continuous improvement. I consistently work on developing my relationship-building skills, always looking for ways to expand my conversation toolkit with new questions and approaches. Just as importantly, I regularly refine my value proposition based on what I learn about others' needs and challenges. This ongoing process of learning and adaptation ensures that my networking efforts become more effective and meaningful over time.

Remember, the foundation phase is not a race. It's a methodical process of building something that will support your professional growth for years to come. Just as a well-built foundation can support a structure for generations, properly established professional relationships can sustain your career through countless changes and challenges.

The key is to remain patient, strategic, and selective. Not every connection needs to be pursued, not every group needs to be joined, and not every invitation needs to be accepted. Your time and energy are precious resources—invest them wisely in building foundations that will truly support your professional goals.

The Art of Listening and Empathy: Beyond Hearing to Understanding

In a world where everyone is eager to speak, the ability to truly listen has become a rare and precious skill. We've all experienced those networking conversations where our "listener" is clearly just waiting for their turn to talk, mentally rehearsing their elevator pitch while we share our thoughts. Their eyes dart around the room, scanning for more "important" connections, while their staged questions feel pulled from a networking script rather than genuine curiosity. This approach isn't just ineffective—it's the antithesis of real relationship building.

The Difference Between Hearing and Listening

Hearing is a physical act. Listening is an art form. When we merely hear, we collect words and sentences, but when we truly listen, we engage in a complex dance of attention, interpretation, and understanding. This distinction is crucial in professional relationships, where the subtleties of communication often carry more weight than the literal words spoken.

Components of Active Listening

Top 5 tips for mastering active listening:

1. Give the speaker your undivided attention and observe nonverbal cues.
2. Use open body language and verbal affirmations to convey engagement.
3. Paraphrase key points to confirm understanding and retain information.
4. Ask clarifying questions, when necessary, but avoid hijacking the conversation.
5. Provide thoughtful responses that demonstrate reflection on the speaker's ideas.

By focusing on these core tips and making active listening regular practice, you can significantly enhance the quality and impact of your professional networking interactions.

The Power of Empathetic Questions

The questions we ask reveal the depth of our listening. Scripted networking questions ("What do you do?" "How long have you been in business?") often leads to scripted answers. But questions born from genuine listening create opportunities for real connection and understanding.

From Script to Authentic Curiosity

Instead of approaching conversations with a mental checklist of questions, allow your natural curiosity to guide you. *I love this word "curiosity", it is who I have been since I was a little girl. Everyone has a story and purpose in life and my curiosity is natural in these environments.*

When someone mentions they've been in their industry for twenty years, rather than immediately asking about their role, you might wonder:

- What changes have they witnessed?
- What keeps them passionate about their field?
- How has their perspective evolved over time?

These questions emerge naturally from actual listening rather than pre-planning.

The Art of Follow-Up Questions

Mastering the art of follow-up questions is crucial for transforming conversations into meaningful connections. Thoughtful follow-ups demonstrate genuine interest, encourage others to elaborate on their experiences, and provide a natural flow to the dialogue. By asking open-ended questions that build upon previous responses, you create space for people to share more nuanced aspects of their stories and perspectives. Well-timed and insightful follow-ups can uncover valuable details, reveal common ground, and spark new ideas for collaboration. They also convey active listening and a sincere desire to understand the other person's unique journey. Crafting skillful follow-up questions is a powerful tool for deepening rapport, uncovering shared interests, and laying the foundation for enduring professional relationships.

Tips for crafting effective follow-up questions:

1. Listen attentively to identify key points or themes to explore further.
2. Ask open-ended questions starting with "how," "what," or "why" to encourage elaboration.
3. Build upon previous responses by referencing specific details they shared.
4. Use phrases like "tell me more about..." or "what was that experience like for you?" to invite deeper reflection.
5. Avoid interrupting or shifting the topic abruptly; allow for thoughtful pauses.
6. Show genuine curiosity and interest in their unique story and perspective.
7. Balance inquiry with sharing your own relevant experiences to foster mutual understanding.
8. Pay attention to nonverbal cues and adjust your questions accordingly.
9. Express appreciation for their insights and vulnerability to reinforce trust.
10. Conclude by summarizing key takeaways and expressing enthusiasm for staying connected.

By incorporating these tips, you can elevate your follow-up questions to create more substantive, memorable conversations that form the basis for meaningful professional relationships.

Creating Conversational Flow Through Empathy

True empathy in professional conversations isn't about simply understanding someone's position, it's about creating an environment where genuine exchange can flourish. This requires a delicate balance of attention, responsiveness, and authentic engagement.

Elements of Empathetic Conversation

1. Present Moment Awareness

- Stay focused on the current exchange rather than planning your next statement
- Notice when the conversation naturally deepens or becomes more meaningful
- Be willing to follow interesting tangents rather than forcing a predetermined path
- Recognize opportunities for genuine connection

2. Emotional Intelligence in Action

- Mirror the speaker's energy level appropriately
- Acknowledge emotions without trying to fix them
- Share relevant experiences when appropriate
- Create space for vulnerability and authenticity

3. Building on Shared Understanding

- Reference previous points in the conversation
- Connect different threads of discussion
- Identify common ground and shared experiences
- Build bridges between different topics

Moving Beyond Traditional Networking Scripts

The greatest barrier to effective listening often comes from our own networking habits and fears. We've been conditioned to believe that every professional conversation needs to lead somewhere specific—a sale, a referral, a partnership. This goal-oriented mindset can blind us to the genuine opportunities for connection that arise naturally in conversation.

Breaking Free from Networking Habits

The most powerful networking moments come when we release our grip on rigid agendas and predetermined outcomes. I've learned to enter each conversation with an open mind and heart, allowing relationships to unfold naturally rather than forcing them toward specific goals. By focusing on genuine understanding rather than achievement, I've discovered that real value emerges organically from authentic connections. This approach requires trust in the process and faith that meaningful opportunities will surface through genuine interaction.

The key to creating lasting professional relationships lies in embracing authentic exchange. Rather than following a scripted approach, I share relevant experiences and insights as they naturally arise in conversation. By allowing my genuine personality to shine through and remaining open to surprise, I've found that conversations often lead to unexpected and valuable destinations. There's a unique joy in discovering new perspectives and allowing others to see the real person behind the professional facade.

Perhaps most importantly, this approach requires practicing patience. I've learned to resist the common urge to rush toward solutions or immediately offer services. Instead, I embrace the power of silence and reflection in conversations, giving space for deeper thoughts and genuine insights to emerge. By allowing relationships to develop at their own pace and trusting in the process of natural connection, I've built stronger, more meaningful professional relationships that stand the test of time.

Remember, the goal of listening isn't to gather information you can use later—it's to create understanding in the present moment. When we listen with genuine curiosity and empathy, we not only learn more about others but also create the foundation for lasting professional relationships built on mutual respect and understanding.

The most valuable connections often come from conversations where we forgot we were networking and simply engaged in genuine human interaction. By mastering the art of listening and empathy, we transform networking from a transaction-focused activity into an opportunity for meaningful connection and mutual growth.

Building Trust and Authenticity: The Heart of Lasting Connections

Trust (n.): The firm belief in the reliability, truth, ability, or strength of someone or something. But in professional relationships, trust is more than its dictionary definition—it's the invisible currency that makes every meaningful connection possible. It's what transforms a business contact into a trusted advisor, a networking acquaintance into a valued colleague, and a casual connection into a lifelong professional ally.

Authenticity (n.): The quality of being genuine, real, and true to one's own personality, spirit, or character. In networking, authenticity means showing up as your whole self, not just your carefully curated professional persona.

The Architecture of Trust

Trust isn't built through grand gestures or single interactions—it's constructed gradually through consistent, authentic behavior and reliable actions.

Understanding the components of trust helps us consciously build it in our professional relationships.

5 Building Blocks to Build Trust

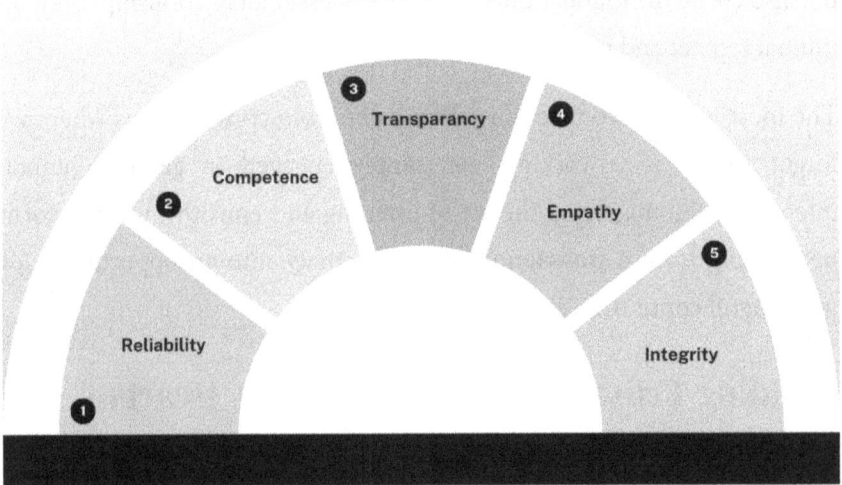

RELIABILITY

- Do what you say you'll do
- Be consistent in your communication
- Follow through on commitments
- Maintain professional boundaries
- Respect others' time and energy

COMPETENCE

- Know your field thoroughly
- Be honest about your limitations *don't say you can do everything, if you can't deliver*
- Continuously develop your skills
- Share knowledge generously

TRANSPARENCY

- Be clear about your intentions
- Communicate openly about challenges
- Share relevant information freely
- Address concerns directly
- Maintain appropriate confidentiality

EMPATHY

- Show genuine concern for others
- Understand others' perspectives
- Recognize and respect feelings
- Demonstrate emotional intelligence
- Support others in challenging times

INTEGRITY

- Maintain consistent values
- Act ethically even when costly
- Keep commitments
- Protect confidential information
- Put relationships before transactions

The Art of Being Real

Authenticity in professional relationships doesn't mean sharing everything or ignoring professional boundaries. Instead, it means being genuine within appropriate parameters. It's about finding the sweet spot between being completely guarded and oversharing.

Navigating this balance requires a nuanced approach. On one hand, sharing personal hobbies, family life, or non-work passions can humanize you and create genuine connection points. Revealing that you enjoy hiking on weekends or volunteering at a local animal shelter can showcase dimensions of your personality that build rapport and trust. These glimpses into your life outside of work can make you more relatable and memorable.

However, it's crucial to maintain clear professional boundaries. Oversharing personal details, discussing sensitive topics, or blurring the lines between work and personal life can undermine your credibility and make others uncomfortable. The key is to share selectively and strategically - offering insights into your life that enhance connection without compromising professionalism.

Remember, authenticity isn't about baring your entire soul - it's about strategically revealing dimensions of yourself that foster trust, rapport, and meaningful connection. Master this balance, and you'll be well on your way to crafting relationships that are both professionally enriching and personally fulfilling.

Elements of Professional Authenticity

1. Genuine Interest in Others

- Show curiosity about people's lives beyond their work
- Remember personal details shared in previous conversations
- Follow up on important life events
- Share in others' celebrations and challenges
- Connect on shared interests and experience

2. Natural Communication Style

- Use your own voice, not business jargon
- Share stories that reveal your personality
- Express genuine emotions appropriately
- Allow your sense of humor to show
- Speak from personal experience

3. Honest Self-Presentation

- Represent your abilities accurately
- Share both successes and learning experiences
- Admit when you don't have answers
- Be open about your professional journey
- Show genuine enthusiasm for your work

Creating Space for Real Connection

Building trust and authenticity requires creating environments and moments where genuine connection can occur. This often means moving beyond traditional networking venues and creating opportunities for more natural interaction.

Strategies for Deeper Connection

Building strong professional relationships flourishes when we vary our interaction settings beyond traditional networking environments. I've found that meeting in different environments and engaging in shared activities creates a more natural foundation for connection. By participating in community events together and creating opportunities for casual interaction, we develop a deeper understanding of each other through shared experiences. These varied settings allow relationships to develop more organically and authentically than they might in formal business environments alone.

Meaningful engagement goes beyond routine interaction to create real value in professional relationships. I actively share relevant resources and opportunities that align with others' goals and interests. When challenges arise, I offer genuine support, and I make it a point to authentically celebrate others' successes. By connecting people with shared interests and actively contributing to others' growth, I help create a network of mutual support and development. This approach to engagement transforms traditional networking into a collaborative community focused on collective success.

The Courage to Be Real

Perhaps the most challenging aspect of building authentic professional relationships is finding the courage to be genuinely ourselves in a business world that often rewards conformity. People want us to be honest and somewhat transparent, they are reading us just as much as we are reading them. Being real is going to be tough for some when they have been taught to put on their business face and stick to a script. Relax…we are all human! We are all part of a community, culture and have the same purpose in mind when it comes to being successful.

Remember, building trust and authenticity is not about following a formula—it's about being consistently real, reliable, and genuine in your professional relationships. It's about creating connections that go beyond business cards and LinkedIn profiles to touch the human elements that make meaningful relationships possible.

Nurturing Relationships for the Long Term: The Unexpected Journey of Connection

When I first began my networking journey, I could never have predicted where these relationships would lead. Writing this book wasn't on my radar. Leading women's professional groups wasn't part of my initial plan. The beautiful truth about genuinely nurturing professional relationships is that they often lead us down paths we never could have imagined for ourselves. They open doors we didn't even know existed and create opportunities that surpass our original goals.

The Magic of Long-Term Relationship Investment

Think of relationship nurturing like tending a garden. You plant seeds, provide consistent care, and sometimes wait seasons before seeing the full bloom. But when those relationships flourish, they create an ecosystem of opportunities, support, and growth that sustains itself and continues to surprise you with unexpected bounty.

The Compound Effect of Genuine Connection

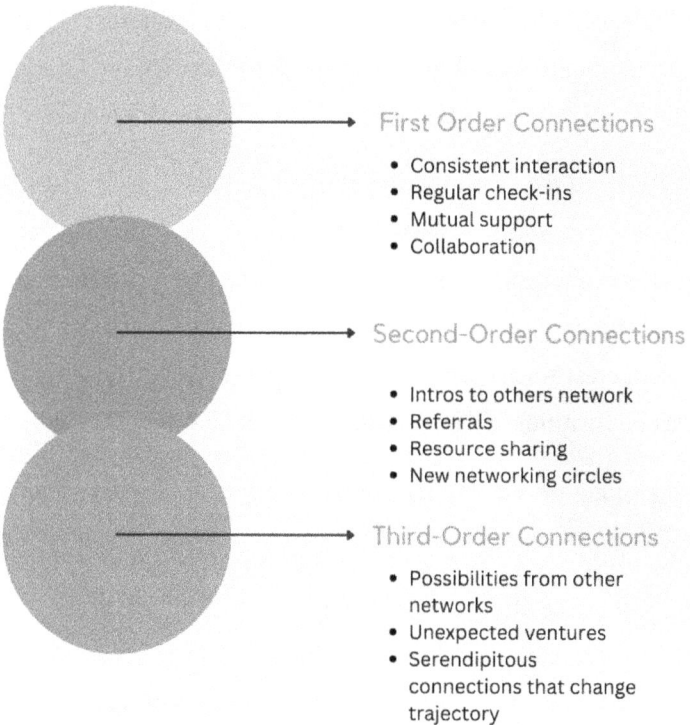

COMOUND EFFECT

First Order Connections
- Consistent interaction
- Regular check-ins
- Mutual support
- Collaboration

Second-Order Connections
- Intros to others network
- Referrals
- Resource sharing
- New networking circles

Third-Order Connections
- Possibilities from other networks
- Unexpected ventures
- Serendipitous connections that change trajectory

1. First-order connections, showing direct relationships with strong, solid connection lines
2. Second-order connections, represented by slightly smaller nodes with dashed lines showing the network extension

3. Third-order opportunities, shown as smaller nodes with dotted connections to represent emerging possibilities

Real-World Connection Examples: The Power of Natural Networking

The Compounding Effect of Event Leadership: A Story of Organic Growth

A powerful example of how event leadership creates unexpected opportunities unfolded after a women's business event I hosted. The event itself was impactful, featuring three women business owners sharing their authentic journeys—both struggles and victories—to an audience of over 70 women. But the real magic happened in the ripple effects that followed.

The very next day, while supporting two panelists (an HR Consultant and a Lender) at another discussion, I experienced the unexpected reward of quality event production. Charlotte, a stylist who had attended my women's event the previous evening, approached me with a collaboration proposal. Her interest wasn't random—it was sparked by witnessing firsthand how I created meaningful connections and valuable experiences for attendees.

This single interaction has blossomed into multiple layers of opportunity and connection:

- Successfully collaborated on a sold-out event
- Developed a deep friendship and ongoing mastermind partnership
- Connected Charlotte with my speaker bureau
- Supported her evolution into corporate speaking about style's role in professional connection
- Created regular strategic planning sessions together

The progression of this relationship demonstrates how authentic leadership and quality event execution can:

- Attract like-minded professionals
- Create collaborative opportunities
- Foster deep professional friendships
- Open doors for mutual growth
- Generate ongoing value exchange

Key Elements That Made This Connection Flourish:

- Quality event execution that showcased expertise
- Being present and accessible at industry events
- Openness to new collaborative opportunities
- Consistent support of others' growth
- Regular investment in the relationship

What makes this story particularly powerful is how one well-executed event led to a cascade of opportunities that continue to expand. Charlotte's journey from event attendee to collaborator to speaker demonstrates how authentic networking creates exponential growth opportunities for everyone involved.

This connection exemplifies the compound effect of genuine networking—how being consistently present, delivering value, and supporting others' growth creates relationships that evolve in unexpected and rewarding ways.

The Art of Long-Term Nurturing: A Personal Journey

Consider the story of Kim, a seasoned corporate professional and business coach, and how an unexpected encounter at a business conference demonstrated the power of genuine connection. At an event where I was representing a mortgage company's employee benefit program, I initially seemed out of place among the other vendors. Kim approached my table with skepticism, questioning the relevance of a mortgage company at a business conference.

As I explained our unique value proposition, something shifted. What began as a brief, potentially dismissive interaction transformed into a meaningful dialogue. Despite our seemingly different backgrounds and professional focuses, we discovered a mutual interest in supporting professionals and businesses.

Our connection didn't follow a predetermined script. Instead, it evolved organically. Over time, we collaborated on workshops and training classes, both in-person and virtual. We became supporters of each other's events, and now we're even co-writing a book – a testament to the unexpected paths genuine relationships can take.

Sustainable relationship nurturing isn't about maintaining a rigid schedule of check-ins or forcing interactions. It's about creating genuine touchpoints that maintain connection while allowing relationships to evolve naturally.

Sustainable Nurturing Practices

Meaningful Follow-Through	Authentic Engagement	Value Creation
• Remember and reference previous conversations • Follow up on important milestones and challenges • Share relevant opportunities and resources • Celebrate others' successes sincerely	• Stay genuinely interested in others' journeys • Share your own evolution and learning • Be present during interactions • Allow relationships to deepen naturally	• Look for ways to contribute to others' success • Share insights and learning experiences • Connect people with complementary needs • Offer support during challenges

The Extraordinary Returns of Patient Investment

The most amazing aspect of long-term relationship nurturing is how it creates opportunities you never could have planned for. My own journey is testament to this truth. What began as simple networking has blossomed into leadership roles, mentoring opportunities, business partnerships, and now, the chance to share these insights through this book.

The Unexpected Benefits

UNEXPECTED BENEFITS

PROFESSIONAL EVOLUTION	• New career directions • Leadership opportunities • Speaking engagements • Advisory roles • Publishing opportunities
PERSONAL GROWTH	• Expanded perspectives • Deeper self-awareness • Enhanced communication skills • Greater emotional intelligence • Increased confidence
COMMUNITY IMPACT	• Ability to help others • Creation of new opportunities • Building supportive networks • Mentoring relationships • Legacy creation

The Journey Continues

The beauty of nurturing long-term professional relationships is that the journey never really ends. Each connection has the potential to lead to new adventures, opportunities, and growth. The key is to remain open to possibilities while consistently investing in genuine relationship building. I will share later how these techniques have connected so many dots and created many opportunities in my life. At times I still can't believe where the journey has led.

Embracing the Unknown

Maintaining genuine curiosity is the cornerstone of meaningful professional relationships. My journey has taught me that staying deeply interested in others' paths opens doors to unexpected opportunities. This curiosity isn't a calculated strategy—it's an authentic approach to understanding the rich, complex narratives of fellow professionals. By approaching each interaction with fresh eyes and sincere interest, I've discovered that the most profound connections often emerge from moments we least expect.

Take, for example, my encounter with Kim, a seasoned business coach I met at a professional conference. What began as a chance interaction at my mortgage company's vendor table—where I initially seemed out of place—transformed into a deep, unexpected partnership. Our connection defied conventional networking logic, proving that genuine curiosity can bridge seemingly disparate professional worlds.

Professional growth becomes exponential when we commit to continuous learning and adaptation. I've made it a priority to learn from others' experiences while openly sharing my own evolving journey. This approach transforms networking from a transactional exercise into a dynamic, mutually enriching process. By embracing new challenges and remaining adaptable, I've found that each connection becomes a potential catalyst for unexpected opportunities.

The most valuable relationships transcend immediate professional gains. I focus on creating a legacy that extends beyond momentary interactions—actively helping others on their professional journeys and sharing the lessons I've learned. This approach transforms networking from a series of brief exchanges into a meaningful contribution to professional community growth. Every genuine connection becomes a thread in a larger tapestry of collective success.

Embracing the unknown is an art form, requiring a unique blend of courage, curiosity, and radical openness. Where others see uncertainty as a threat, I've discovered it as a canvas of infinite possibilities. The most transformative moments of my professional journey have emerged from unexpected intersections—chance conversations that sparked collaborative ventures, serendipitous meetings that reshaped entire career trajectories. Each unplanned detour has been a masterclass in professional growth, revealing that the most remarkable paths are rarely the ones we meticulously map.

By nurturing relationships with authenticity and patience, we create a network of possibilities that continues to surprise and delight us. Every conversation, every genuine interaction carries the potential to open doors we never knew existed.

The journey from networking novice to trusted connector, from business card collector to community builder—these transformations happen through the patient, genuine nurturing of authentic relationships. Time and again, life has shown me that embracing the unknown isn't just worthwhile—it's where the real magic of professional growth happens.

My experience with Michele is a testament to this truth. We first connected while serving together on the board of Upward Women, a women's non-profit group in Las Vegas. At the time, I had no idea that the person sitting next to me would become my most trusted business coach and a pivotal guide in establishing Jayde Consulting in 2022.

What drew me to Michele was her unique perspective. I knew I needed someone who could challenge my thinking, someone who could provide insights that would push me beyond my comfort zone. Her background in the hospitality industry, marked by numerous professional accolades, brought a fresh approach to business strategy that was fundamentally different from my own. As she too had decided to branch out and support entrepreneurial owners, our connection felt almost predestined.

Michele's coaching style was precisely what I needed—direct, insightful, and unafraid to challenge my assumptions. She became more than just a coach; she became my go-to resource for critical business decisions. Whether I'm navigating complex professional challenges or contemplating strategic moves for Jayde Consulting, Michele offers the kind of perspective that transforms potential obstacles into opportunities for growth.

Our connection exemplifies the true essence of meaningful professional networking. It's not about collecting contacts or exchanging business cards. It's about finding those rare connections that challenge you, support you, and help you see your professional journey from entirely new angles. Michele has been instrumental in helping me refine my vision, question my approaches, and ultimately, build a more robust and thoughtful business.

This journey of connection is fundamentally about developing what I call a magnetic presence—an authentic confidence that attracts opportunities and inspires others. In the chapters ahead, I'll dive deep into how we cultivate this powerful personal brand. It's more than just external perception; it's about internal growth, understanding your unique value, and showing up authentically in every professional interaction.

Just as Michele helped me see beyond my initial limitations, developing a magnetic presence is about peeling back layers of self-doubt and revealing the most genuine, powerful version of yourself. It's about transforming how you see yourself and how others perceive your potential.

The bridge between meaningful connections and a magnetic presence is authenticity—the ability to be truly, unapologetically yourself while remaining open to growth, challenge, and continuous learning.

CHAPTER 2

Developing a Magnetic Presence: The Power of Authentic Confidence

A magnetic presence isn't about being the loudest in the room or wearing the most expensive suit—it's about cultivating an authentic confidence that draws people to you naturally. Through my years of networking and leading women's professional groups, I've learned that true magnetism comes from the perfect alignment of how you present yourself externally and how you feel internally.

Authentic Assurance: Building Presence from Within

Your presence begins long before you enter a room. It starts with how you feel about yourself and your value. When I first started networking, I focused entirely on external factors—what to wear, what to say, how to stand. While these elements matter, I quickly learned that without internal confidence, no amount of external polishing would create the presence I desired.

Imagine you're an explorer, setting out each day to chart new territories and make fascinating discoveries. Your confidence is like your trusty compass - it guides you through unfamiliar terrain, helps you make sense of your surroundings, and keeps you oriented towards your goals.

But where does this inner compass come from? How do you cultivate a sense of direction that's uniquely your own? It starts with a deep understanding of yourself and your own value.

Picture your life experiences, skills, and perspectives as a vibrant tapestry, woven from countless unique threads. Each thread tells a story - a challenge you've overcome, a lesson you've learned, a talent you've honed. As you step back and survey this rich tableau, you begin to see how each thread contributes to the overall masterpiece that is you.

Perhaps there's a bold red strand representing a time you faced a fear and emerged stronger. A shimmering gold filament might symbolize a moment of profound insight or personal growth. A sturdy blue cord could signify a skill you've mastered through dedication and practice.

As you examine your tapestry, you start to appreciate the value of each thread, and how they combine to create a one-of-a-kind work of art. You understand that your perspective is shaped by a constellation of experiences that no one else shares. This realization is the foundation of authentic confidence - a deep-seated belief in your own worth and the unique gifts you bring to the world.

But developing this confidence isn't about achieving perfection or erasing your flaws. In fact, it's quite the opposite. True confidence comes from embracing your whole self, imperfections and all.

As you navigate the uncharted territories of your professional journey, remember that true confidence comes not from having all the answers, but from being comfortable with the questions. It comes from owning your story, valuing your perspective, and trusting that your unique threads are exactly what the world needs.

Mastering Your Professional Image

While internal confidence is fundamental, how we present ourselves matters. Professional polish isn't about conforming to rigid standards—it's about expressing your authentic self in a way that makes others comfortable and confident in your capabilities. I've learned that this includes:

Thoughtful Personal Presentation

Your appearance should make you feel confident while being appropriate for your industry and role. This doesn't mean sacrificing your personality—it means understanding how to express it professionally. I've found that when I feel comfortable and confident in my appearance, it naturally enhances my presence.

Body Language That Invites Connection

Your physical presence communicates volumes before you speak a word. I practice:

- Open posture that welcomes interaction
- Genuine smile that reaches the eyes
- Engaged eye contact that shows interest
- Relaxed but professional stance
- Gestures that emphasize rather than distract

The Power of Personal Brand Consistency

In today's interconnected world, your professional presence must seamlessly bridge the gap between in-person interactions and digital platforms. Think of your personal brand as a promise you make to your professional community—it needs to deliver the same experience whether someone meets you at a networking event, connects with you on LinkedIn, or follows your professional journey online.

When people encounter the same genuine enthusiasm, professionalism, and value-driven approach across all platforms, they develop unwavering confidence in who you are and what you represent. For instance, if I'm known for being a passionate connector and community builder in person, my social media presence should reflect this through regular posts about successful connections made and community events supported.

Aligning your online and offline presence is about honoring the trust people place in you. Ensure your in-person interactions reflect what you post about, whether it's being a relationship-focused business developer or sharing networking insights. Consistently demonstrating your principles across all platforms creates a powerful ripple effect, allowing your reputation to precede you positively.

The key is ensuring that whether someone first encounters you through social media or meets you in person, they experience the same authentic professional presence that defines your brand.Remember, in an age where people often research you online before meeting in person, any disconnect between your digital presence and real-world behavior can damage your credibility. Your personal brand should be a genuine reflection of who you are, consistently expressed across all platforms and interactions.

The Energy You Bring: A Case Study in Authentic Professional Growth

Michael's journey is a powerful illustration of how maintaining authentic enthusiasm and core values can transform a professional path. When I first met him in 2016, he was an emerging massage therapist on the brink of opening his own practice, balancing the challenges of building a business while supporting a young family.

What sets Michael apart is his unwavering commitment to his core values. Unlike many professionals who compartmentalize their personal and professional lives, Michael integrates them seamlessly. He consistently demonstrates that success isn't just about business achievements, but about creating a life that aligns with one's deepest priorities. By deliberately blocking out time for family and sharing those moments openly, he shows that professional success and personal fulfillment can coexist.

His professional evolution is nothing short of inspiring. From a solo massage therapist to a multi-faceted entrepreneur, Michael has expanded his impact by coaching others in his industry. The creation of the BadAss Planner for Massage Therapists, Spa, and Service Providers is a testament to his innovative spirit and commitment to supporting fellow professionals.

The BadAss Planner is more than just a productivity tool—it's a manifestation of Michael's philosophy. Designed to ensure professionals take necessary daily steps towards their goals, the planner embodies his belief that success is about consistent, intentional action. As he puts it, the planner is crafted to make goals not just possible, but inevitable.

What truly stands out is Michael's ability to build a business that provides both professional success and personal freedom. His capacity to take extended family vacations while maintaining a thriving business speaks volumes about his strategic approach to work-life integration. He doesn't just preach balance—he lives it.

Michael's journey reminds us that authentic professional growth is about more than just achieving business milestones. It's about staying true to your core values, continually learning, and creating a professional life that supports your most important personal priorities.

Your energy signature is a magnetic force that attracts or repels others. Authentic enthusiasm is irresistibly attractive in professional settings. When you genuinely light up discussing your work or celebrate others' successes sincerely, that energy becomes contagious, strengthening relationships. It's not about fake excitement, but radiating your natural passion in every interaction.

The Impact of Authentic Presence

When you cultivate an authentically confident presence, infused with the radiance of your inner worth and polished with the gleam of your external expression, you become a magnet for meaningful connections and transformative opportunities.

At events and gatherings, people will gravitate towards you, eager to bask in the warmth of your confident energy. They'll seek out your insights, your ideas, and your unique perspective, recognizing the value you bring to every conversation.

Your magnetic presence will leave an indelible mark on those you encounter. People will remember the way you made them feel - heard, understood, and inspired. They'll recall the clarity of your communication, the intentionality of your presence, and the depth of your engagement.

As your reputation grows, opportunities will begin to seek you out, drawn to the magnetic force of your confident, capable presence. Your inbox will fill with invitations, your phone will buzz with exciting propositions, and your path will be illuminated with possibilities that align with your unique talents and aspirations. This is the power of a magnetic presence - it not only attracts success but also creates a gravitational field that pulls you towards your most fulfilling potential.

The Art of Story Based Introductions

Let me share how I transformed my professional introduction from a rehearsed elevator pitch into a compelling story that naturally draws people in. The turning point came when I realized that people connect with stories, not sales pitches. Instead of leading with my title or role, I now begin with a brief story that illuminates why I'm passionate about what I do.

For instance, when meeting new people, I might start by sharing, "You know that feeling when you meet someone and instantly know they could help solve a problem for someone else in your network? That spark of excitement when you can connect two people who need to know each other? That's what drives me every day. I've been orchestrating these connections since 2016, watching businesses grow and professionals thrive through the power of strategic relationship building."

This storytelling approach accomplishes several things simultaneously. It creates an emotional connection, demonstrates my passion authentically, and naturally leads into a conversation about how I help others. By sharing a relatable moment or feeling, I invite others to see themselves in the story. This opens the door for them to share their own experiences, turning what could have been a one-sided pitch into an engaging dialogue.

The key is keeping your story concise while making it memorable. Think about a moment that crystallizes why you do what you do. Maybe it's the client whose business transformed after a connection you made, or the moment you realized your true professional calling. When you share this kind of authentic story, you create what I call a "curiosity bridge" – people naturally want to know more, leading to deeper, more meaningful conversations.

Remember, your introduction should feel like the beginning of a conversation, not the end of one. By using story instead of a pitch, you create space for others to engage, ask questions, and share their own experiences. This approach transforms the traditional networking introduction from a transaction into an invitation for genuine connection.

Common Mistakes to Avoid

Your personal brand is the lasting impression you leave in every room, conversation, and interaction—not just what you post online or your job title. Through years of networking and leading professional women's groups, I've learned that a powerful personal brand is built through consistent actions and authentic relationships, not carefully curated digital personas.

When crafting your professional image and presence, it's crucial to avoid the pitfall of trying to imitate others or pretending to be someone you're not. Mimicking another's style might feel like a shortcut to success, but it ultimately undermines your authenticity. Instead, focus on developing your own genuine presence that aligns your external image with your internal identity. Embrace what makes you uniquely you and let that shine through in your interactions.

Another common pitfall is allowing nerves or discomfort to manifest in your body language. Anxiety can make us fidget, cross our arms defensively, or avoid eye contact—all signals that can undermine the confident image we want to project. To counter this, try grounding techniques before high-pressure situations: take deep breaths, roll your shoulders back into a posture of assuredness, and visualize yourself exuding calm confidence. Bring yourself fully into the present moment before engaging. By practicing these techniques, you can train yourself not just project confidence regardless of any internal butterflies.

Remember - building an influential personal brand is an inside-out process. By aligning your outward presence with your inner authenticity and managing your mindset in challenging situations, you create a powerful, consistent impression that sets you apart genuinely rather than superficially. Honing this skill will make you magnetic not just in high-visibility moments but in every interaction that shapes how others perceive & remember you.

Have No Fear

Let me share a story that perfectly illustrates the power of pushing past hesitation and seizing opportunity in the moment. When I attended an event at Allegiant Stadium with my friend Tracy, whose brother was a sponsor, I had no idea it would lead to an incredible connection. The featured speaker was a former NFL player, and as I listened to his inspiring presentation and the Q&A that followed, I noticed something interesting: despite his impressive NFL career and clear speaking talents, he mentioned future aspirations that suggested he didn't have representation for corporate speaking opportunities.

Most people might have thought, "Surely a former NFL player already has all the connections he needs," or "Who am I to approach someone of his caliber?" But I've learned that magical opportunities often come from being brave enough to take action when others hesitate. So after his talk, I approached him directly and asked if he had an agent for corporate speaking engagements. To my surprise, he didn't! That simple moment of courage—pushing past any intimidation I might have felt about approaching a former NFL player—led to a valuable connection and the opportunity to help guide his next chapter. This experience reinforces what I've learned: sometimes the biggest opportunities come from being bold enough to simply ask.

The Power of Follow-Through

The connection didn't end with our conversation. By taking his book "The IF in Life" and tagging him on Instagram, I created a natural follow-up opportunity. His response via DM requesting guidance about other projects was both humbling and exciting. The fact that an NFL player sought my direction speaks volumes about:

- The value of business development expertise
- The importance of authentic connection
- The universal need for strategic guidance
- The power of showing genuine interest

- The impact of taking initiative

Key Lessons from This Connection:

1. Accept unexpected invitations
2. Stay alert for opportunities
3. Have courage to approach anyone
4. Ask the obvious questions
5. Follow through consistently
6. Remain humble and helpful

This experience reinforces that you truly never know where a simple "yes" to an invitation might lead, or what doors might open when you simply gather the courage to ask. The biggest opportunities often come from taking those small steps that others might hesitate to take.

The Power of Following Up

The difference between a forgettable interaction and a meaningful professional relationship often comes down to what happens after your first meeting. Let me share a story that perfectly illustrates the power of authentic follow-up and long-term relationship nurturing.

When I first met Landon, a business financial advisor, our connection wasn't built on business prospects—it centered on his excitement about becoming a father to twins. Instead of launching into a typical networking conversation, I focused on this personal milestone, even gifting him a 'New Dad' t-shirt. This genuine interest in his personal life laid the foundation for what would become a five-year strong professional relationship and counting and he just had his third baby, clearly I am in constant contact with him.

The key to maintaining this connection wasn't complicated—it was about consistency and authentic interest. Through regular quarterly lunch meetings, I earned the nickname "follow-up queen." These weren't agenda-driven meetings focused on business opportunities; they were genuine check-ins about both his professional journey and personal growth. This consistent follow-up created a deep level of trust and understanding that no single networking event could achieve.

The true power of this approach revealed itself recently during a podcast interview with Landon. When he mentioned needing a project manager, I immediately connected the dots to another professional in my network who was seeking exactly that role. This perfect match would never have happened without the foundation of regular check-ins, active listening, and genuine curiosity about others' journeys. It wasn't forced networking—it was the natural result of maintaining authentic relationships.

Perhaps the most telling sign of successful follow-up is when it creates natural reciprocity. Today, Landon consistently asks how he can help me—not because he feels obligated, but because genuine relationships naturally evolve into mutual support. This is what happens when follow-up comes from a place of authentic interest rather than strategic networking tactics.

The lesson here is clear: effective follow-up isn't about checking boxes or maintaining superficial connections. It's about creating genuine relationships that stand the test of time and generate unexpected opportunities for everyone involved. Whether you're following up after a first meeting or maintaining long-term professional relationships, the key ingredients remain the same: authenticity, consistency, and genuine interest in others' success.

The Long-Term Impact

Think of a powerful first impression as planting a seed that will grow into a mighty professional relationship. I've seen that those initial moments of connection lay the groundwork for everything that follows. When done thoughtfully, this first interaction creates a foundation of trust and opens pathways for meaningful professional relationships to develop naturally over time.

Consider how a well-crafted first impression acts like a preview of your professional brand story. When I meet someone new, I aim to give them a genuine glimpse of who I am and what they can expect from our professional relationship. This isn't about presenting a polished facade—it's about authentically demonstrating your values and approach to business relationships. For instance, if I'm known for being a connector and relationship builder, I might naturally weave a story about a successful connection I recently facilitated into our first conversation, showing rather than telling what I bring to professional relationships.

The true measure of a successful first impression reveals itself in what happens next. When both parties leave an interaction genuinely looking forward to future engagement, you've created what I call a "connection bridge"—a natural pathway to deeper professional relationship building. This anticipation for future interaction stems from establishing authentic trust during that first meeting. It's like creating a professional promise that says, "What you see is what you'll continue to get from me." This consistency between first impression and ongoing interactions builds the kind of reliability that sustains long-term professional relationships.

Remember, every strong professional relationship in your network began with that crucial first impression. By approaching these initial interactions with intention and authenticity, you create the foundation for relationships that can grow and evolve over years, bringing unexpected opportunities and value to all involved. The goal isn't just to make people remember you—it's to make them look forward to knowing you better.

Your first impression is your brand's introduction to the world. Make it count not by being perfect, but by being authentically engaged, genuinely interested, and intentionally present in each new connection you make.

The Essence of Personal Branding

Your personal brand transcends social media posts and business card titles. It's the genuine impression you create in every room, conversation, and interaction. Through years of networking and leading professional groups, I've discovered that a powerful personal brand emerges from consistent, authentic actions—not from carefully curated online personas.

True personal branding is about showing up authentically, demonstrating your values through everyday interactions, and building meaningful relationships that reflect your genuine self. It's less about crafting an image and more about living your professional truth consistently and transparently.

Your Professional Value: A Holistic Approach to Excellence

Building a Reputation That Lasts

A strong reputation isn't built overnight—it's the result of consistent actions over time. Focus on:

- Being known for something specific
- Delivering consistent quality
- Following through on commitments
- Supporting others' success
- Contributing to your professional community

Remember, your personal brand isn't what you say about yourself—it's what others say about you when you're not in the room. Build it through consistent, authentic action and genuine value creation, and your reputation will become one of your most powerful professional assets.

Focus on building a brand that reflects your true professional self, adds value to your community, and creates a legacy of positive impact in your industry. When your personal brand authentically reflects who you are and what you stand for, it naturally attracts the right opportunities and relationships to support your professional growth.

But authentic branding is just the beginning. In the next chapter, I'll dive deep into the strategic art of networking—showing you how to transform your authentic presence into meaningful, efficient connections. You'll discover how to move beyond the exhausting approach of trying to be everywhere and meet everyone, to a targeted, purposeful networking strategy that maximizes your time and energy.

We'll explore techniques to:

- Quickly assess the potential of networking opportunities
- Distinguish between different types of professional connections
- Create a strategic approach that allows you to make the most of every interaction
- Develop a system that prevents networking burnout while expanding your professional ecosystem

The journey from developing an authentic personal brand to becoming a strategic networker is about intentionality—understanding that every connection is an opportunity, but not every opportunity is worth pursuing. It's about working smarter, not harder, and creating a networking approach that feels natural, genuine, and ultimately transformative.

CHAPTER 3

Streamline Your Networking Approach: Efficient Techniques to Boost Connections

Early in my networking journey, I made the classic mistake many of us do—I tried to be everywhere, meet everyone, and pursue every possible connection. I would spend hours at networking events, collecting business cards like they were rare trading cards, only to find myself exhausted and overwhelmed with follow-up tasks that rarely led to meaningful results. It wasn't until I learned to approach networking with strategic clarity that I began to see real returns on my time investment.

The Power of Strategic Clarity

One of my most significant breakthrough moments came during a particularly busy month of networking. I was serving as chapter president for one women's group while actively participating in another, attending three to four events monthly. Despite my packed calendar, I wasn't seeing the results I wanted. That's when I realized I was treating every conversation the same way, regardless of whether I was speaking with a potential client or a possible referral partner.

Distinguishing Your Audience

Success in networking requires understanding that not all connections serve the same purpose. Through years of experience, I've identified three primary categories of professional connections:

3 Types of Audiences

Potential Clients/Customers	Referral Partners	Community Builders
• Direct beneficiaries of your services • Those with immediate needs • People within your target • Individuals who match your ideal client profile	• Complementary service providers • Industry connectors • Centers of influence • Strategic allies	• Event organizers • Group leaders • Industry advocate • Mentors and advisors

The Art of Initial Assessment

I've learned to quickly assess which category someone falls into within the first few minutes of conversation. This isn't about being dismissive—it's about being efficient and respectful of everyone's time. Here's my personal approach:

The Three-Minute Strategy

1. Listen for Need Indicators

- Current challenges
- Future goals
- Immediate pain points

2. Identify Alignment Opportunities

- Service overlap
- Target market similarities
- Collaborative potential

3. Gauge Engagement Level

- Conversation depth
- Question quality
- Follow-up interest

Maximizing Event Effectiveness

Through years of trial and error, I've developed a system that helps me make the most of any networking event:

Pre-Event Strategy

A successful pre-event strategy begins with careful event selection. This involves researching attendee demographics to ensure the right audience match, reviewing the event format and structure to understand participation opportunities, considering timing and location efficiency to maximize attendance, and evaluating the potential return on time investment to ensure it aligns with your goals.

Goal setting forms the next crucial phase of preparation. This includes defining specific objectives for what you want to achieve at the event, setting realistic targets for the number and quality of connections you aim to make, planning effective conversation strategies to engage with others, and preparing any relevant resources you might need to support your objectives.

Finally, energy management plays a vital role in ensuring your success at the event. This encompasses scheduling events strategically to avoid burnout, planning adequate recovery time between networking activities, preparing both mentally and physically for the engagement, and setting clear boundaries about your time and involvement. By managing your energy effectively, you can maintain peak performance throughout the event and maximize your networking outcomes.

The Time Investment Matrix

One of my most valuable lessons has been learning to allocate my networking time strategically. I now use what I call the Time Investment Matrix:

Initial Meeting Time Allocation

Potential Clients (30-45 Minutes): Making Every Minute Count

Deep Dive into Their Needs (First 10-15 Minutes)

I always open with questions that reveal what's really driving their search for solutions. For example, when meeting with a business owner struggling with growth, I might discover that their real need isn't just more clients—it's creating systems that allow them to serve more clients without burning out.

Thorough Exploration of Challenges (Next 10-15 Minutes)

This is where we unpack the obstacles standing in their way. Recently, a client shared they weren't getting results from networking events. Through careful questioning, we uncovered that they were attending plenty of events but had no follow-up system in place. The real challenge wasn't event attendance—it was relationship maintenance.

Detailed Discussion of Solutions (Next 10-15 Minutes)

Once we understand the true challenges, we can explore potential solutions. For instance, with the business owner struggling with growth, we discussed implementing specific tools and strategies for automating certain processes, allowing them to scale without sacrificing quality.

Clear Next Steps (Final 5-10 Minutes)

This crucial phase ensures the meeting leads to action. I always end with specific, actionable items. Example:

- Schedule a follow-up strategy session
- Share relevant resources within 24 hours
- Connect them with specific people in my network who can help
- Outline the first three steps they need to take

Referral Partners (20-30 Minutes): Creating Strategic Alliances

Mutual Opportunity Exploration (First 10 Minutes)

This is where we discover how our businesses naturally complement each other. For example, when I met with a business financial advisor, we explored how his work with business owners' finances dovetailed perfectly with my expertise in business development. We identified specific client scenarios where our services would create a comprehensive solution.

Clear Value Proposition Exchange (Next 5-10 Minutes)

During this phase, we clearly articulate what we each bring to the table. For instance, when meeting with a real estate agent, she explained her focus on luxury residential properties, while I shared how my network includes many executives relocating to Las Vegas. This clarity helped us understand exactly when and how to refer to each other.

Partnership Potential Assessment (Final 5-10 Minutes)

This is the strategic planning phase where we determine if and how we'll work together. I recently met with a corporate trainer, and during this segment, we:

- Identified specific types of clients to refer to each other
- Created clear criteria for qualified referrals
- Established preferred communication methods
- Planned joint networking opportunities

Each successful referral partnership I've built, from CPAs to HR consultants, has followed this structured approach while allowing room for authentic connection to develop.

Community Connections (15-20 Minutes): Building the Network Web

Quick Value Exchange (First 8-10 Minutes)

This is the perfect time to identify mutual interests and potential ways to support each other in the community. For example:

- When I met the director of a local non-profit, we quickly identified how my network could support their upcoming fundraiser
- During a chat with a chamber of commerce member, we discovered overlapping interests in women's leadership development

- Meeting with a local tech meetup organizer led to immediate opportunities for speaker exchanges

Future Touchpoint Planning (Final 5-10 Minutes)

This crucial phase establishes how we'll stay connected and add value to each other's community efforts. Real examples include:

- Setting up quarterly coffee meetings to share community updates
- Planning to attend each other's upcoming events
- Creating a schedule for cross-promoting community initiatives
- Identifying specific ways to support each other's organization

The key is to make these interactions efficient yet meaningful. For instance, I recently met with a women's group leader, and in just 15 minutes, we:

- Shared our upcoming event calendars
- Identified three ways to cross-promote
- Set up a system for sharing relevant opportunities
- Scheduled our next connection point

Personal Success Stories

Let me share a story that illustrates the power of this strategic approach. At a chamber event last year, I met someone who initially seemed like a potential referral partner. Following my three-minute assessment strategy, I quickly realized she was actually an ideal client. By adjusting my conversation approach in real-time, what could have been a pleasant but ultimately unproductive referral partner meeting turned into a significant client relationship that has since led to multiple projects.

Another time, I almost missed a valuable connection because I initially misidentified their category. They seemed like a direct client, but through careful listening, I realized they were actually a powerful referral partner who has since become one of my strongest allies in the business community. This taught me the importance of staying flexible and alert to shifting dynamics even within my strategic framework.

The Evolution of Strategy

Your networking strategy should evolve as your business grows and your goals change. Mine certainly has. What worked when I was building my initial client base needed to shift as I moved into leadership roles and began focusing on larger initiatives. The key is to maintain clear objectives while remaining adaptable to new opportunities.

In-Person Networking: Finding Your Authentic Style

The myth that successful networking requires an extroverted personality has held back countless talented professionals. Through my years of leading diverse networking groups, I've watched both extroverts and introverts excel in their own unique ways. The key isn't becoming someone you're not—it's learning to leverage your natural strengths while developing strategies to manage your challenges.

Understanding Your Networking Style

Before diving into specific tips, it's essential to understand that neither extroversion nor introversion is inherently better for networking. Each brings its own strengths and challenges to the table. As an extrovert, I have found many in the room are introverted and once I realized that I knew I had to change my approach.

The Natural Extroverted Networker's Toolkit

As someone who thrives on human connection, I've learned to harness my natural networking abilities while being mindful of potential blind spots.

Let me share how I've learned to leverage these traits effectively in professional settings.

Our Natural Strengths

Think of extroverted networkers like myself as the spark plugs in professional gatherings. We often:

- Light up rooms with natural enthusiasm and energy
- Break the ice in group settings without hesitation
- Form connections as naturally as breathing
- Navigate networking events like fish in water
- Create dynamic, engaging conversations on the fly

This natural ability to generate energy and connection is like having a superpower in the networking world. I've found that my ability to easily engage with others often helps create an environment where even more reserved professionals feel comfortable joining conversations.

Growth Opportunities

However, with great energy comes great responsibility. Over the years, I've learned to be mindful of certain tendencies that could impact relationship building:

- Balancing my enthusiasm with active listening
- Ensuring each interaction has depth beyond surface connection
- Paying closer attention to subtle communication cues
- Being mindful of others' energy levels and engagement preferences
- Focusing my networking efforts strategically rather than trying to connect with everyone

Understanding these aspects has helped me develop a more balanced approach. For instance, I now consciously create pauses in conversations, allowing others to fully express their thoughts. I've learned to channel my natural enthusiasm into creating inclusive conversations rather than dominating them.

The key is leveraging our natural social energy while remaining mindful of how it affects others. This awareness transforms us from simply being social butterflies into strategic relationship builders.

The Introverted Networker: Mastering the Art of Meaningful Connection

While networking events might seem designed for extroverts, introverted professionals possess unique strengths that create some of the most powerful and lasting business relationships. Through my years of leading professional groups, I've witnessed how introverted networkers excel at building deep, meaningful connections that often lead to the most valuable long-term partnerships.

The Introvert's Natural Networking Gifts

These professionals are like master composers, creating harmony through carefully orchestrated interactions:

- They listen with remarkable depth, catching nuances others might miss
- Their responses carry weight, showing careful consideration of each conversation
- One-on-one interactions become opportunities for genuine connection
- They notice subtle patterns and opportunities others overlook
- When they commit to follow-up, it happens with purpose and precision

I've watched introverted networkers transform seemingly casual conversations into powerful professional relationships simply through their ability to truly hear and understand others' needs.

Navigation Points for Introverts

Understanding how to work with your introverted nature rather than against it is key to networking success:

- Managing energy levels requires strategic planning for networking events
- Finding natural entry points into group conversations takes practice
- Building in dedicated recovery time between networking activities
- Balancing the desire for meaningful dialogue with networking time constraints
- Creating comfortable spaces within busy networking environments

The key isn't changing your introverted nature but embracing it strategically. For instance, arriving early to events can provide quieter opportunities for connection, and scheduling one-on-one follow-up meetings plays to your strength of deeper conversations.

Success in networking isn't about being the loudest voice in the room—it's about making each interaction count. Introverted networkers excel at creating lasting impact through genuine, focused engagement.

Universal Success Strategies

Regardless of personality type, certain strategies work for everyone:

Pre-Event Strategy: Your Networking Game Plan

Along the way I've learned that successful networking events don't start when you walk through the door—they begin with thoughtful preparation.

Let me share how I approach pre-event planning to maximize every networking opportunity.

First, I do my homework. Whenever possible, I review the attendee list or research the typical audience for the event. This isn't about stalking LinkedIn profiles—it's about understanding who I might meet and identifying potential connections that could add value to both parties. Recently, before a chamber event, I noticed several business owners would be attending who could benefit from connecting with each other. This advanced knowledge helped me facilitate meaningful introductions during the event.

Next, I set clear, achievable goals for each event. Instead of vague objectives like "meet new people," I might aim to have three meaningful conversations about specific topics or connect two people who could benefit from knowing each other. These focused goals help me stay strategic rather than scattered. Having a few key topics in mind helps me navigate conversations naturally while adding value. I like to say I know a little bit about a lot—not because I'm an expert in everything, but because I'm genuinely curious and retain key insights from every professional I meet.

Energy management is crucial. I plan my schedule around networking events, ensuring I'm at my best when I attend. This might mean blocking off time before for preparation and after for follow-up, or scheduling lighter workloads on networking days. I plan my events like they are a business meeting so I do not overbook myself for any networking days I have planned.

Finally, I'm selective about which events I attend. Not every networking opportunity is the right opportunity. I choose events that align with my goals and where I can add value to others. Quality always trumps quantity when it comes to building meaningful professional relationships.

Your Event Success Strategy: Making Every Minute Count

Success at networking events isn't just about showing up—it's about showing up strategically. Through countless events since I've attended, I've developed an approach that keeps me energized, effective, and authentically engaged throughout each event.

I always arrive with what I call my "connection mindset." This means walking in with genuine enthusiasm for the possibilities ahead. It's not about working the room—it's about being open to discovering how I might help others or learn something new. This positive energy is contagious and often leads to more meaningful interactions.

Rather than trying to meet everyone, I focus on making a few quality connections. My goal might be to have three substantial conversations or to help connect two people who could benefit from knowing each other. These achievable targets keep me focused and prevent that overwhelming feeling of trying to do too much.

Most importantly, I stay true to my natural networking style. Whether you're naturally outgoing or more reserved, authenticity builds trust. People can sense when you're putting on an act, so I focus on being genuinely myself while being professionally appropriate.

The Art of Strategic Follow-Up

Let me share a hard truth I've learned through years of networking: a stack of business cards collecting dust on your desk might as well be confetti. The real magic of networking doesn't happen during that first handshake or initial conversation—it happens in the follow-up. I've watched countless professionals attend event after event, collect dozens of cards, and then wonder why their network isn't growing. The answer is simple but often overlooked: they've mastered the art of meeting people but failed at the science of following up.

The Critical Window of Opportunity

The 48 hours following a networking event are golden. I learned this lesson early on, when I noticed a clear pattern: connections I followed up with quickly became lasting professional relationships, while those I delayed contacting often faded into the abyss of missed opportunities. This isn't just about being prompt—it's about showing respect for the connection and maintaining the momentum of that initial meeting.

My post-event ritual begins the moment I leave. While conversations are fresh in my mind, I make quick notes about key discussions and promised actions. I'll be honest most of these notes end up on a post-it note that I keep in my car, then it goes into my database. I note specific ways I can add value, whether it's making an introduction or sharing a relevant resource. There is usually a connection I will be making for them in the next 24 hours. I will reference specific conversation points and include any promised resources or introductions. For example, if someone mentioned struggling with social media strategy, I'll send them an introduction to a social media expert in my network.

Following Up with Purpose

Effective follow-up isn't just about sending a generic "Great to meet you" email. It's about continuing the conversation in a meaningful way that demonstrates your genuine interest and adds value.

When crafting your follow-up message:

- Reference specific points from your conversation
- Include any promised resources or connections

- Suggest a clear next step or action item
- Make it personal and authentic

For example, after meeting Sarah, a business coach struggling with client acquisition, my follow-up email included a reference to our discussion about her unique coaching approach, an introduction to a podcast host looking for guest experts, and a suggestion for a coffee meeting to explore collaboration opportunities.

Building Long-Term Relationship Systems

Success in follow-up requires more than good intentions—it demands a systematic approach. Here's my proven system for maintaining meaningful professional relationships:

The Three-Tier Follow-Up Framework

1. Immediate Connections (48-Hour Focus)

- LinkedIn connection
- Thank you email
- Resource sharing
- Initial meeting scheduling

2. Short-Term Nurture (First Month)

- Coffee meeting or virtual catch-up
- Relevant article sharing
- Strategic introductions
- Opportunity identification

3. Long-Term Relationship Building (Ongoing)

- Quarterly check-ins
- Birthday/anniversary acknowledgments

- Event invitations
- Collaboration opportunities

The key is turning those initial connections into ongoing relationships. Every strong relationship in my network started with intentional, thoughtful follow-up after that first meeting.

The Long-Term View: Nurturing Your Network for Lasting Success

In the fast-paced world of professional networking, it's easy to get caught up in the buzz of the moment - the thrill of a successful conference, the rush of a promising new connection, the satisfaction of a well-received follow-up message. However, the true value of networking lies not in these fleeting instances, but in the long-term relationships they have the potential to create.

This long-term approach to networking can feel daunting, especially in a culture that often prioritizes quick wins and immediate returns. It requires patience, persistence, and a genuine commitment to helping others succeed. But the payoff is immense.

Some of the most transformative opportunities in my own career have come not from one-off encounters, but from relationships nurtured over years. A casual conversation at a conference led to an invitation to speak at an event months later. A follow-up email sparked a collaboration that spanned several projects. A long-standing connection became a trusted mentor during a career transition.

And remember, this long-term approach is not just a strategy for professional gain - it's a mindset of generosity, a commitment to lifting others up as you climb. By focusing on how you can contribute to your network's success over time, you create a ripple effect of positive impact that extends far beyond your own career.

Leveraging Social Media for Networking Success: Finding Your Digital Voice

Let me start with a confession: I am not a social media guru. Like many professionals, I initially resisted the idea that I needed to maintain an active social media presence. However, through my networking journey, I've learned that social media isn't optional in today's professional landscape—it's an essential extension of your networking strategy. The good news? You don't have to be an expert to leverage it effectively.

The Reality of Digital Presence

In today's interconnected world, your social media presence often serves as your first impression. Before someone meets you at a networking event, speaks with you on a call, or considers doing business with you, they're likely to look you up online. This reality forced me to shift from viewing social media as an optional extra to seeing it as a crucial component of my professional presence.

Building Your Digital Foundation: Where Real Connections Begin

LinkedIn stands as the cornerstone of my professional online presence. As my favorite and most utilized platform, it has become my digital networking home base. The power of LinkedIn lies not just in what you share, but in the genuine connections it can create. Let me share a perfect example.

One day, I received a connection request from Jamila who is a speaker, coach and business consultant. Now, many people might have simply accepted the request and moved on, but I've learned that sometimes the most meaningful relationships start with a simple LinkedIn message. Jamila and I quickly discovered we shared similar passions and perspectives about business and community. What started as a digital connection blossomed into a true friendship and powerful professional partnership. We've since hosted and facilitated numerous events together, creating impact we couldn't have achieved individually.

This experience reinforces why LinkedIn is so much more than just another social media platform—it's a gateway to real, meaningful professional relationships. When someone reaches out through LinkedIn, I take notice. You never know which connection might lead to your next great collaboration or friendship.

Beyond LinkedIn, I maintain a strategic presence on industry-specific platforms that align with my professional goals. While I don't try to be everywhere, I focus my energy on platforms where my target audience naturally gathers. This focused approach ensures my digital networking efforts remain both efficient and effective, creating meaningful connections rather than just collecting followers.

The key is being intentional with your platform choices and consistent in your engagement. Each platform should serve a specific purpose in your overall networking strategy, with LinkedIn serving as your professional home base. And remember—behind every connection request might be your next great professional partnership.

The Power of Consistency Over Perfection

One of my biggest lessons was understanding that consistency matters more than perfection. Whether you are able to maintain regular posting schedules or use platforms to do so, you can also maximize your time by outsourcing certain aspects of my social media presence. There is not a shortage of Social Media Managers out there.

Working Smart: Leveraging Tools for Consistency

Being effective on social media isn't about doing everything yourself—it's about knowing where you add unique value and working smart with the tools available. I've learned to combine authentic engagement with strategic automation.

I take a realistic approach to social media management. LinkedIn is my sweet spot—I love engaging directly with my network, sharing insights, and building authentic connections. Let me be real with you about my content creation process. While many experts recommend using voice notes or fancy apps to capture content ideas, I stick to good old-fashioned Post-it notes. You'll find them everywhere—in my car, on my desk, in my purse, stuck to my computer monitor. When inspiration strikes, whether it's from a client meeting, a networking event, or just a random thought, I grab the nearest Post-it and jot it down.

Is it the most sophisticated system? Nope. Is it technically efficient? Probably not. But it works for me, and that's what matters. These little yellow squares become the foundation for my social media content. Some might become LinkedIn posts about a successful connection I helped create, others transform into longer pieces about networking strategies, and some simply remind me to celebrate someone else's success.

The key isn't having the perfect system—it's having a system that you'll actually use consistently. Sometimes the simplest solutions are the most effective, even if they're not the most recommended.

To maintain consistency without becoming overwhelmed, I utilize scheduling tools like Hootsuite or Co-Scheduler. These platforms allow me to batch-create content when I'm feeling inspired and schedule posts for optimal timing. For instance, I spend once a month scheduling my content, freeing me to focus on genuine engagement during busy workdays.

Building genuine relationships and adding real value to my network—while ensuring my social media presence remains professional and consistent. The key is finding the right mix of personal touch, smart automation, and professional support that works for your schedule and style.

Maximizing LinkedIn for Professional Networking

The Power of Active LinkedIn Engagement

I am nowhere near being a LinkedIn expert but I've discovered that LinkedIn's true power lies not just in posting content, but in genuine engagement with your network. It's about being present, being interested, and being involved in others' professional journeys. When someone in my network shares a win, lands a new role, or launches a new venture, I'm there with genuine congratulations and encouragement.

Think of LinkedIn as a virtual networking event that never ends. Just as you wouldn't stand in a corner at an in-person event, you shouldn't be passive on LinkedIn. I make it a point to comment meaningfully on posts, share insights on others' content, and celebrate their milestones. This isn't just about being nice—it's about building real relationships and showing consistent support for your professional community.

The best part? Most of these engagement tools are completely FREE. You don't need a premium account to have meaningful interactions or build strong connections. Simple actions like thoughtful comments, sharing others' content with your perspective, or posting congratulations on achievements can create significant impact. These small but consistent actions show you're genuinely interested in others' success, not just focused on promoting yourself.

Remember, the most successful networkers don't just talk about themselves—they actively participate in their community's conversations and celebrations. Your engagement on LinkedIn should reflect the same authenticity you bring to in-person networking.

Authenticity Unleashed: Your Digital Networking Superpower

In the crowded digital realm of LinkedIn, where countless professionals vie for attention, authenticity emerges as the ultimate networking superpower. I've witnessed firsthand how people can effortlessly detect and dismiss manufactured engagement from afar. That's precisely why I infuse my personal touch into every piece of content I share and every interaction I have, ensuring that my true self shines through.

Sharing my entrepreneurial origins is a passion of mine, and I relish the opportunity to showcase not just who I am today, but the roots from which my business acumen sprouted. Imagine this: an adorable snapshot of a young me, sitting proudly at my little desk, diligently creating handmade checks for my pretend business ventures. These throwback moments aren't merely a nostalgic indulgence; they serve as a testament to the entrepreneurial spark that has been kindling within me since the beginning.

In stark contrast, picture another childhood photo: baby me, face scrunched up and wailing, clutching a phone in my tiny hands. That image perfectly encapsulates my early fear of phone calls, a far cry from the confident salesperson I am today, always ready to hop on a call and close a deal. By vulnerably sharing these personal glimpses into my journey—the highs and the lows, the triumphs and the fears—I invite my network to connect with the authentic me, not just a polished professional facade.

When I share updates about the events I'm attending or hosting, it's an in-the-moment, unfiltered expression of my genuine excitement. Imagine me at a women's leadership event, snapping a quick photo and sharing the inspiration that's coursing through me at that very instant. These authentic shares provide my network with a window into my professional world and the communities I'm deeply invested in.

The stories I share aren't meticulously crafted marketing messages; they're authentic accounts of my lived experiences along my networking journey. When I recount a successful connection I helped forge or a valuable lesson gleaned from a networking event, it's driven by a sincere desire to empower others to learn and grow from these experiences.

Janelle Kennedy · You

Keynote Speaker | Business Growth Strategist | Podcast Host | Ve...

2w · 🌐

Someone asked me today when I started in my sales journey. I originally said when my mom had an Avon route in 1978 that I took over and ran for her at the age of 8 (I was in entrepreneurial heaven).

But looking at this photo, which was in 1975, it began much earlier. I was always thinking about what businesses and creating whatever I could dream up. I sit at my desk writing this post, much like the desk in this photo. Some things never change!

Thanks to my parents for allowing me to be me and always encouraging me to do what I was passionate about!

Always remember, your LinkedIn presence should be a seamless extension of your in-person persona. Your network isn't connected with a meticulously curated brand; they're engaging with the authentic you, your unique journey, and the story that has shaped you from the very beginning—the budding entrepreneur at her little desk and the scared baby learning to face her fears.

In essence, authenticity is the secret sauce that transforms your digital networking from a mere transactional exchange to a genuine, meaningful connection. By fearlessly embracing your true self and sharing your journey with vulnerability and candor, you create an irresistible magnetic pull that draws others to you. So, let your authenticity shine through in every post, every comment, and every interaction, and watch as your digital networking superpower propels you to new heights of success and fulfillment. Get ready to set the LinkedIn world ablaze with the fire of your unfiltered realness.

You never know who's watching your professional journey unfold on social media. While we often measure engagement through likes, comments, and shares, some of our most impactful connections come from silent observers—those who follow our content without actively engaging. It's a reminder that genuine value reaches far beyond the metrics we can measure.

Let me share a perfect example of this. When I increased my video presence on LinkedIn, I had no idea who was really paying attention. Then one day, Francesca, a real estate agent I'd known for years, reached out. Though she had never liked or commented on my posts, she had been quietly following my content evolution and was genuinely curious about the changes in my business approach. What began as a simple conversation about social media strategy transformed into something far more meaningful.

During our discussion, I practiced what I preach about active listening and being fully present. When Francesca mentioned her interest in public speaking, I immediately recognized an opportunity to add value. Because I maintained strong relationships with a speaker bureau, I was able to make a connection that could help her achieve her goals. This initial conversation evolved naturally into a mentoring relationship, with me coaching her through her career transition and helping define her next professional steps.

This experience taught me a valuable lesson about professional visibility: your impact often extends far beyond what you can see. While some connections actively engage with your content, others silently absorb your insights, waiting for the right moment to reach out. That's why authenticity in your professional presence is so crucial—you never know who might be drawing inspiration or insight from your shared journey.

The beauty of this connection lies in how organically it developed. While most people focus on creating content for visibility's sake, the real power comes from using that visibility to spark authentic conversations and uncover hidden opportunities. By maintaining an active and genuine presence on LinkedIn, staying attuned to others' needs, and being ready to add value at any moment, we create a foundation for meaningful professional relationships to flourish.

This approach to strategic connection building isn't about forcing relationships or manufacturing opportunities. It's about being consistently present, genuinely interested, and always ready to add value when the moment presents itself. Whether through social media or in-person interactions, the key is to focus on building authentic connections that can evolve naturally over time.

Integration with In-Person Conference Networking

Creating Synergy: Maximizing Networking Opportunities Before, During and After Events

1. Pre-Event Connection

- Research the attendee list ahead of time and strategically connect with key people you want to meet.
- Share across your social media channels that you will be attending or speaking at the event. Tag the event organizers and use the official event hashtag to boost visibility.
- Directly engage with posts from the event organizers to demonstrate your enthusiasm and begin building those relationships early.

2. Strategic Participation

- During networking breaks and meals, sit with new people each time. Introduce yourself and ask questions to learn about their work and goals. Listen intently and find ways to support them.
- Post photos, key takeaways, and tag people you meet. This keeps your network engaged from afar and shows your commitment to learning and connecting.
- Be a connector at the event, introducing people to each other as you discover aligned interests or goals. Being a superconnector who facilitates meaningful new relationships will make you highly valuable and memorable to others.

3. Post-Event Follow-Up

- Within 24 hours of the event, send a personalized follow-up message to each person you met, big or small. Recap your conversation, share any links or resources you promised, and suggest a next step for building the relationship, such as a call or coffee chat.

- Post an event recap on LinkedIn sharing your top takeaways. Tag abundantly to create exposure for yourself, the event, and your new connections.

By deploying this strategic three-part approach to networking at events, you will maximize every opportunity for visibility, credibility and relationships. Connecting before, engaging during, and following up after shows your dedication and consistency - highly attractive qualities in any industry. As you implement these tips, your network and influence will grow exponentially, opening doors to opportunities beyond what you ever expected. The key is synergy - the more you connect others and add value, the more it will come back to you tenfold. Get ready to uplevel your networking game and watch your career soar to new heights.

Online Networking: The Digital Dynamic

The Evolving Landscape of Online Networking

In recent years, virtual networking has not only become increasingly important, but has undergone a significant transformation in its role and prevalence. While online interaction has long been a valuable supplement to in-person networking, the events of 2020 catalyzed a seismic shift in how we connect professionally.

This rapid digitalization of networking brought both challenges and opportunities. On one hand, the lack of in-person interaction made it harder to build rapport and forge deep connections. The serendipity of bumping into a colleague at a conference coffee break or bonding over drinks at a post-event mixer was notably absent.

On the other hand, virtual networking democratized access in an unprecedented way. Suddenly, geography was no longer a barrier -

professionals could connect with counterparts across the globe as easily as across the street. Introverts and those with mobility challenges found new opportunities to engage on their own terms. And the cost and time savings of not having to travel opened up networking to a much broader range of participants.

The New Networking Equilibrium

In day-to-day networking, many are maintaining the digital habits built up over the past few years. Quick Zoom chats are replacing some coffee meetups, community engagement is staying strong even as in-person activity resumes, and the global connections forged in the pandemic era are being nurtured across time zones.

One of the key advantages of virtual networking is its efficiency. Without the need for travel, professionals can engage in a greater number of interactions in a shorter span of time. A day that might have previously accommodated one or two in-person meetings can now be filled with a variety of virtual touchpoints - from quick one-on-one video chats to larger group sessions and webinars.

So lean into the new norm of virtual connection, but don't lose sight of the enduring value of face-to-face engagement. Approach your professional relationships with a spirit of openness, flexibility, and purposeful communication, and you'll be well-equipped to build a network that supports and propels you, no matter what the future of networking holds.

Key Takeaways

- Strategic networking is about quality over quantity
- Different connections require different approaches
- Effective follow-up is crucial for relationship building
- Digital presence enhances in-person networking

- Consistency and authenticity matter across all platforms

Remember, effective networking isn't about working harder—it's about working smarter. By understanding who you're talking to and what you're working toward, you can make every networking interaction more meaningful and productive. The goal isn't to minimize connections but to maximize their potential for mutual benefit.

But what does true contribution really mean? In the next chapter, we'll dive deep into the often-misunderstood concept of value in professional relationships. You'll discover that value extends far beyond simple transactions or service offerings. It's about transformation—understanding how you can genuinely enrich someone's professional and personal journey. As we move from the mechanics of networking to the art of value creation, you'll learn how to transform connections into meaningful partnerships that drive success for everyone involved.

CHAPTER 4

Title: Focus on Value: Redefining Professional Connections

Let's talk about one of the most misunderstood concepts in professional relationships: value. Too often, professionals limit their understanding of value to their product features or service offerings. They recite their capabilities like a menu, thinking this alone demonstrates value. But after years of building deep professional relationships, I've learned that true value extends far beyond what you sell or what you do—it encompasses every way you can enrich someone's professional and personal journey.

4 Dimensions of Professional Value

Value isn't a transaction—it's a transformation. Through my networking experiences, I've discovered that true value manifests in four critical dimensions:

1. Knowledge and Insight Sharing

This goes beyond simply passing along industry news; it's about offering perspective that helps others see their challenges in a new light. When I share experiences from my own journey or connect dots that others might miss, I'm not just providing information—I'm offering insights that can transform how someone approaches their business challenges.

2. Strategic Connections

The power of thoughtful connections represents a crucial value dimension. I've learned that making introductions isn't just about connecting two people—it's about creating possibilities that neither party might have imagined on their own. When I connect complementary businesses or build bridges between industries, I'm orchestrating opportunities for collaboration that can transform businesses and careers.

The Unexpected Path of Strategic Connections

Sometimes, the most transformative professional relationships emerge from connections made years earlier. Take my experience with David, a former employer from my home warranty representative days. Years after we had last worked together, he reached out with a purposeful introduction to Coby and Gina, a mortgage broker team he was coaching.

David's recommendation wasn't just a casual referral. He specifically described me as "a connector in town," recognizing my ability to create meaningful professional relationships. What seemed like a simple introduction would become a pivotal moment in my professional journey.

Our initial meeting was more than a standard networking interaction. Coby and Gina were looking for ways to enhance their selling process, and my background in business development and networking perfectly aligned with their needs. What began as a potential connection quickly evolved into a multifaceted professional relationship.

First, they became clients of my title business. But the connection didn't stop there. Nine months later, I found myself working directly with them in business development, bringing my network and strategic connection skills to significantly improve their selling process.

This story demonstrates the compound effect of authentic networking. A connection made years earlier, rooted in mutual respect and recognition of professional value, can lead to opportunities that neither party could have anticipated. It wasn't about immediate gain, but about the potential for mutual growth and support.

The key elements that made this connection remarkable:

- Long-term professional reputation
- Willingness to make meaningful introductions
- Recognizing potential beyond immediate circumstances
- Openness to evolving professional relationships

3. Personal Support

Though often overlooked, personal support provides immense value in professional relationships. Being present for others during both challenges and triumphs creates a depth of connection that transcends typical business interactions. Whether serving as a sounding board for new ideas or offering emotional intelligence during difficult business situations, this type of support builds trust and creates lasting bonds.

4. Business Growth and Strategic Development

This dimension focuses on more than just spotting opportunities—it's about seeing potential synergies and helping others maximize their business potential. By sharing market insights, suggesting efficiency improvements, and identifying strategic opportunities, we help others expand their vision of what's possible.

Together, these dimensions of value create a comprehensive approach to professional relationship building. When we understand and actively engage in all these areas, we transform networking from a transaction-focused activity into a powerful force for mutual growth and success.

Case Studies in Value Creation

My journey in industry discussions crystallized during a local business banker's event where I encountered Andrew, the Economic Forecast Director from UNLV. This encounter wasn't just another networking moment – it was the beginning of a strategic knowledge-sharing partnership.

Instead of treating Andrew's presentation as a passive learning experience, I recognized something more profound: the incredible value his expertise could bring to a broader professional community. My approach was deliberate and purposeful – to create a win-win-win scenario that would benefit multiple stakeholders.

Through strategic facilitation, I began creating speaking opportunities that brought Andrew's economic insights to diverse professional audiences. The results were remarkable:

- My clients gained direct access to expert economic analysis
- Andrew expanded his reach, consistently speaking to engaged audiences
- I established myself as a valuable connector within the business community

A Real-World Symphony of Connection: Danielle's Story

Sometimes, the magic of networking reveals itself through a beautiful narrative of intuition, trust, and collaborative spirit. Take the story of Danielle, a business development professional at a fractional CFO company, whose networking prowess demonstrates the true art of value creation.

Danielle's connection with her networking partner exemplifies a deep, almost telepathic understanding of professional potential. When she encountered Sheila, a technology industry professional, her intuition immediately sparked. This wasn't just a casual encounter, but a moment of profound recognition—seeing beyond surface-level interactions to the underlying potential for transformative collaboration.

Sheila, navigating the early stages of her business journey, was seeking refined direction and meaningful community connection. Danielle's unique genius lay in her ability to see not just a contact, but a perfect alignment of expertise and opportunity. Her instinct led her to introduce Sheila to a business development consultant who could provide precisely the support and strategic guidance she needed.

The result was nothing short of remarkable:

- Strategic business development consulting provided clear, actionable insights
- Speaking opportunities that expanded Sheila's professional visibility
- Regular strategy sessions that fostered continuous learning and growth
- A platform for sharing forward-thinking technological perspectives
- An ongoing relationship of mutual support and collaborative advancement

The Alchemy of Strategic Networking

This story illuminates the deeper principles of value creation through connection:

Layers of Impact

1. **Intuitive Opportunity Recognition**: The ability to spot perfect alignment between people's needs and capabilities.
2. **Trust as a Foundational Element**: The confidence to make meaningful introductions based on deep professional understanding.
3. **Natural Collaboration**: How the right connection can organically evolve into a rich, multifaceted professional relationship.

4. **Continuous Growth**: The ongoing potential for mutual development that emerges from thoughtful networking.

The Evolution of Personal Connections: From Childhood Friends to Business Partners

While many of our strongest professional relationships begin in business settings, sometimes our most powerful connections have roots that stretch back long before we enter the professional world. My relationship with Nino, a retired North Las Vegas firefighter, perfectly illustrates how deep-rooted personal connections can evolve into unexpected professional opportunities.

What began as a childhood friendship transformed into a professional partnership that exemplifies the true essence of authentic networking. Nino's background in community outreach and event management gave him a unique perspective on building meaningful connections. It was through this lens that he introduced me to Leticia, a mindfulness mentor and consultant who was just beginning her entrepreneurial journey.

The introduction wasn't just a casual referral. Leticia and I immediately connected, discovering a shared passion for empowering professionals through our respective expertise. Our relationship quickly evolved beyond a simple introduction. We became collaborators, frequently sharing stages as public speakers, each bringing our unique insights to audiences seeking personal and professional growth.

Our approach was symbiotic. By deeply understanding our respective clients' needs, we were able to create more impactful presentations and services. This mutual understanding became a cornerstone of our professional relationship, demonstrating how genuine connection goes far beyond surface-level networking.

But the story doesn't end there. Years later, Nino and I found ourselves partnering on a business venture in the non-profit space. What started as a personal relationship had grown into a strategic business opportunity that neither of us could have predicted when we first knew each other.

This journey illustrates several key principles of meaningful networking:

- Personal relationships can become your most powerful professional assets
- Authentic connections often lead to unexpected opportunities
- Long-term relationships create unique collaborative potential
- Your network is a living, evolving ecosystem of possibilities

The magic happens when we approach relationships with genuine interest, openness, and a willingness to support one another's growth. Nino's introduction to Leticia, our speaking collaborations, and our subsequent business partnership are testament to the power of connections that transcend traditional networking approaches.

This evolution from personal friendship to professional collaboration exemplifies the compound effect of relationship investment we'll explore further in this chapter. It shows how connections cultivated with authenticity create ripples of opportunity that continue to expand over time.

Charlotte's Journey: From Attendee to Collaborator

The day after the event, something remarkable happened. While supporting two panelists at another discussion, the organic nature of meaningful networking revealed itself. Charlotte, a stylist who had been in the audience the previous evening, approached with a collaboration proposal.

Her interest wasn't coincidental. She had witnessed firsthand the art of creating valuable, connected experiences—and recognized a kindred professional spirit.

The Anatomy of an Unexpected Connection

This single interaction blossomed into a multi-layered professional relationship:

1. **Collaborative Success**: A sold-out event that combined their unique expertise
2. **Deep Professional Friendship**: An ongoing mastermind partnership
3. **Career Expansion**: Connection to a speaker bureau
4. **Professional Evolution**: Supporting Charlotte's journey into corporate speaking about style's role in professional connection
5. **Continuous Growth**: Regular strategic planning sessions

Decoding the Mechanics of Meaningful Networking

What Transforms a Casual Encounter into a Profound Connection?

Several critical elements converge to create this type of transformative networking:

1. Quality of Execution

- Meticulous event planning
- Creating spaces that invite genuine interaction
- Demonstrating professional expertise through action, not just words

2. Accessibility and Presence

- Being genuinely available

- Showing up fully in professional spaces
- Creating an approachable, supportive demeanor

3. Collaborative Mindset

- Openness to unexpected opportunities
- Viewing connections as potential collaborative journeys
- Removing transactional barriers

4. Consistent Support

- Investing in others' growth trajectories
- Following up and creating ongoing value
- Maintaining genuine interest in professional evolution

Practical Strategies for Adding Value

Developing a "Value Radar"

The art of adding value begins with developing what I call a "value radar"—a heightened sense of awareness that goes beyond surface-level interactions. This isn't a skill you're born with; it's cultivated through intentional practice and genuine curiosity about others.

Key Components of Your Value Radar:

- Active Listening: Move beyond hearing words to understanding underlying meanings
- Contextual Awareness: Recognize the broader professional and personal landscape
- Empathetic Observation: Tune into both spoken and unspoken needs
- Creative Connecting: See potential bridges between people, resources, and opportunities

Practical Exercises to Sharpen Your Value Radar:

1. Pre-Conversation Preparation

- Research before networking events
- Prepare thoughtful questions
- Think about potential ways you might add value

2. During Conversation Techniques

- Ask open-ended questions
- Listen more than you speak
- Take mental (or physical) notes about unique challenges and goals
- Look for intersection points between your network and the person's needs

3. Post-Conversation Reflection

- Review your notes immediately after interaction
- Identify potential resources or connections
- Create a follow-up plan

Identifying Unspoken Needs

Most professionals communicate only a fraction of their true challenges. The magic happens when you can detect the needs lying beneath the surface.

Techniques for Uncovering Deeper Needs:

- Pay attention to language patterns
- Notice what's not being said
- Recognize the emotions behind the words
- Look for subtle hints of struggle or aspiration

Common Unspoken Needs:

- Confidence building
- Strategic guidance
- Emotional support
- Professional validation
- Network expansion
- Skill development

Case Study: Connecting the Dots - Ressel's Transformation

In my consulting work, business owners come to me when they want to expand their reach, elevate their offerings, and gain clarity about their ideal clients. One of the most powerful aspects of my work involves showing clients how to discover opportunities through relationships they already have but haven't fully leveraged for their business growth.

Ressel's story perfectly illustrates the transformative impact of this approach. After attending one of my business development sessions, she immediately applied what we discussed to her situation. Ressel was looking to scale her business and enter a new industry, but wasn't sure where to start. What she needed was insight on who she already knew and how these existing relationships could serve as crucial connection points to reach her goals.

During our work together, we mapped out her current network and identified several key relationships that could open doors to her target industry. The exercise was simple but profound: recognizing the "dots" already present in her life and strategically connecting them to create pathways toward her objectives.

The moment when Ressel began to see these connections was electric. Her expression shifted from uncertainty to excitement as she realized she already possessed many of the relationships necessary to achieve her goals. She just hadn't recognized their potential value.

What brings me the greatest satisfaction in my work is witnessing these transformations. Seeing Ressel methodically implement our strategies and achieve tangible results reinforces why I'm so passionate about this work. She's now successfully expanding into her target industry by leveraging introductions from people already in her network – connections that were there all along, just waiting to be activated.

Ressel's journey exemplifies what happens when professionals stop viewing networking as collecting new contacts and instead focus on deepening and activating the relationships they already have. Sometimes, the most valuable opportunities aren't found through meeting new people, but through seeing your existing relationships through a fresh, strategic lens.

Case Study: The Hidden Need

During a professional conversation with David, a lender, he mentioned he was putting together a program with a group of trust attorneys and financial advisors targeting corporate employees. Instantly, I recognized a potential connection. Amy, an HR specialist I knew, had extensive networks within corporate environments and could help direct them to the right people.

Not long after our conversation, I was thrilled to see David on a panel discussion alongside Amy, presenting to a precisely targeted group. By identifying the unspoken need for strategic connections and corporate access, I was able to facilitate a relationship that perfectly aligned with David's professional objectives.

This interaction exemplifies the power of detecting underlying professional needs. While David was discussing his program, the unstated need was finding the right audience and making meaningful corporate connections. By listening carefully and drawing on my network, I could provide a solution that went far beyond what was explicitly stated.

The case study demonstrates several key techniques for uncovering deeper needs:

- Paying attention to subtle context
- Recognizing potential synergies
- Understanding the broader goals behind surface-level discussions
- Leveraging a diverse professional network

Creating Meaningful Connections

Connection isn't about quantity—it's about quality and intentionality.

Connection Creation Framework:

1. Understand Individual Potential

- See beyond current roles
- Recognize unique strengths
- Imagine future possibilities

2. Matchmaking with Purpose

- Create connections that benefit both parties
- Look for complementary skills and goals
- Think ecosystem, not transaction

3. Facilitate, Don't Force

- Introduce with context
- Provide clear value proposition
- Step back and let relationships develop organically

Consistent Follow-up and Support

The riches are in the follow-up. True value creation is a long-term commitment.

Follow-Up Strategy:

- 24-Hour Rule: Reach out within a day of meeting
- Personalized Communication: Reference specific conversation points
- Value-Add Approach: Always include something helpful
- Consistency: Regular check-ins, not just when you need something

Support Levels:

- Immediate Support: Resources, introductions
- Short-Term Support: Ongoing communication, advice
- Long-Term Support: Mentorship, career development

Tracking and Nurturing Your Network:

- Use a relationship management system
- Set reminders for follow-ups
- Celebrate others' wins
- Be present during challenges

The Compound Effect of Value Creation

Think of your network like a financial investment. Small, consistent deposits of value compound over time, creating exponential returns.

Real-World Example: I once connected Nina, an EOS implementor, with Shanna, a financial advisor. This simple introduction led to:

- Nina gaining a significant client

- Shanna improving her team's effectiveness
- A long-term professional friendship
- Multiple subsequent introductions

The Mindset Shift:

- From "What can I get?"
- To "What can I contribute?"

Potential Pitfalls to Avoid

- Over-promising
- Inauthentic connections
- Keeping score
- Expecting immediate returns
- Networking only when you need something

Measuring Your Value-Add Impact

While value can't always be quantified, you can track:

- Number of meaningful introductions
- Successful collaborations sparked
- Gratitude received
- Personal growth of your network

Remember, the goal isn't to be a perfect connector. It's to approach every interaction with genuine intention, curiosity, and a desire to support others' growth.

Your most powerful networking asset is your capacity to see potential in others and create environments where that potential can flourish.

The Economic Impact of Strategic Connections

Strategic connections are not merely networking opportunities; they represent critical economic leverage points that can significantly transform business performance. The economic impact of these connections manifests through multiple tangible and intangible channels:

1. **Direct Revenue Generation**: Strategic connections can create immediate revenue streams through:

   - Referral partnerships
   - Joint venture opportunities
   - Shared market access
   - Collaborative product development

2. **Cost Optimization**: Effective strategic connections enable substantial cost reductions by:

   - Sharing operational resources
   - Reducing customer acquisition expenses
   - Leveraging collective bargaining power
   - Minimizing redundant infrastructure investments

3. **Innovation Acceleration**: Economic value emerges through accelerated innovation:

   - Cross-pollination of ideas
   - Shared research and development
   - Access to diverse expertise and perspectives
   - Faster market adaptation

4. **Risk Mitigation**: Strategic connections provide economic resilience by:

   - Diversifying market exposure

- Creating alternative supply chains
- Sharing technological and market risks
- Enhancing collective competitive intelligence

5. **Multiplier Effect**: The true economic potential of strategic connections extends beyond immediate, measurable outcomes. Each connection creates a network effect that exponentially increases potential value, transforming individual relationships into a complex, high-value ecosystem.

By understanding and strategically cultivating these connections, organizations can unlock substantial economic potential, turning networking from a passive activity into a dynamic value creation mechanism.

The Long-Term Impact of Authentic Networking

Building a Reputation Ecosystem (visual)

Imagine walking into a professional event and experiencing a remarkable phenomenon: familiar faces light up with recognition, conversations start before you've spoken a word, and your reputation enters the room before you do. This is the profound power of long-term value creation.

The Invisible Network of Remembered Impact

Your professional reputation becomes a living, breathing entity that:

Speaks on your behalf in rooms you haven't yet entered

Creates opportunities through collective goodwill

Establishes you as a gravitational center of professional networks

Layers of Professional Remembrance:

1. Personal Memory

- Individuals recall specific moments of support
- People remember how you made them feel
- Your genuine care becomes a lasting emotional imprint

2. Professional Reputation

- Colleagues describe you as a go-to resource
- Your name becomes synonymous with strategic support
- You're seen as a problem solver, not just a service provider

3. Network Influence

- Your introductions carry inherent credibility
- Others actively seek your perspective
- You become a trusted node in professional ecosystems

The Ripple Effect of Genuine Connections

Consider a scenario where you've helped three professionals over several years:

- Introduced a startup founder to her first investor
- Provided mentorship to a mid-career professional
- Connected a non-profit leader with critical resources

Years later, these individuals don't just remember a transaction—they remember a transformative moment of support.

The Psychological Mechanics of Being Remembered:

- Reciprocity: People naturally want to return kindness
- Trust Amplification: Your reputation becomes social capital

- Network Magnetism: Genuine connectors naturally attract opportunities

Real-World Impact Stories:

1. The Unexpected Mentor A chance introduction I made years ago between a young entrepreneur and an industry veteran led to a mentorship that completely transformed the entrepreneur's business trajectory. Years later, both continue to credit that initial connection as a pivotal moment in their careers.
2. Community Catalyst By consistently supporting local business owners, I've watched a network grow from disconnected individuals to a robust, supportive community that generates opportunities for everyone involved.

Transforming Networking into Collaborative Practice

The Evolution of Professional Connection:

Traditional Networking:

- Transactional interactions
- Focused on immediate gains
- Competitive mindset
- Limited scope of support

Collaborative Networking:

- Holistic relationship building
- Long-term perspective
- Mutual growth
- Ecosystem thinking

Key Principles of Collaborative Networking:

1. Abundance Mindset

- Believe there's enough opportunity for everyone
- Celebrate others' successes
- Share resources generously

2. Intentional Relationship Building

- Quality over quantity
- Deep, meaningful connections
- Consistent, genuine support

3. Ecosystem Thinking

- View your network as an interconnected community
- Create value for the collective
- Recognize interdependence

Practical Strategies for Collaborative Networking:

- Host cross-industry events
- Create knowledge-sharing platforms
- Develop mentorship programs
- Facilitate introductions without expectation
- Invest in others' growth

The Compound Interest of Professional Relationships

Just as financial investments grow through compound interest, professional relationships accumulate value through consistent, intentional nurturing.

Calculation of Network Value:

- Initial Connection: 1x

- First Follow-up: 2x
- Consistent Support: 4x
- Long-Term Collaboration: 8x+

Walking Into the Room: A Metaphorical Transformation

As you cultivate this approach, professional spaces transform. You're no longer entering a room of strangers, but a network you've helped shape—where connections are measured not in business cards exchanged, but in lives meaningfully touched.

The Ultimate Professional Currency: Your most valuable asset becomes your capacity to:

- See potential in others
- Create environments of genuine connection
- Support multidimensional professional growth
- Generate opportunities through authentic leadership

The Philosophical Underpinning

Networking isn't about collecting contacts, it's about:

- Recognizing human potential
- Creating generative professional spaces
- Understanding every interaction's transformative possibility
- Viewing professional growth as a collaborative journey

The Essence of Connection:

In a world often fixated on immediate transactions, you become something rare: a professional catalyst who understands that the most powerful networks are built on genuine support, curiosity, and a commitment to collective elevation.

Your legacy isn't measured by your individual achievements, but by the opportunities you create for others, the connections you nurture, and the communities you help build.

CHAPTER 5

Ditch the Pitch: Moving Beyond One-Dimensional Sales

Now that we've mastered the art of building meaningful connections and creating valuable relationships, let's tackle the part that makes many of us squirm—selling ourselves and our services. After all, what good is a robust network if we can't effectively communicate our value to those who need us most?

Think back to the last time you were sold something. How did that experience make you feel? Now flip that around—remember when you had to sell something yourself? For many of us, that second memory might bring up feelings of discomfort, choppy conversations, or disappointing results. I've been selling since I was 16 years old and through a lot of experience I've learned that selling doesn't have to feel uncomfortable—it can be a beautiful expression of service when it comes from a place of authenticity.

The key is transforming how we view the selling process. Instead of seeing it as pushing our services onto others, we can approach it as an opportunity to solve problems and fulfill needs. When we genuinely understand someone's challenges and know we can help, sharing our solutions becomes a natural extension of our relationship-building process rather than a forced sales pitch.

The Problem with Traditional Pitches

Many of us became business owners because we're passionate about our craft, not because we love selling. Yet we find ourselves focused on talking about:

- Our techniques

- Our materials
- Our processes
- Our certifications

How many of you are currently doing this? I'll bet most, because that is what we have seen, have been trained to do. Times have changed!

Here's the crucial insight: your customers aren't buying your processes or your products. They're buying their dreams—the peace of mind of a reliable car, the joy of a perfect home, the confidence of financial security. I'm not the first one to talk about this, you will continually hear this come from those in the sales industry and will continue to be the new way of selling. We are in a new era, a new generation of buyers and the old school ways aren't as effective any longer. Our approach needs to shift when society shifts.

The Foundation: Integrity, Innovation, and Honesty

The strongest professional relationships are built on three core principles that should guide every sales conversation:

- Integrity: Always doing the right thing
- Innovation: Looking at problems from different angles
- Honesty: Being clear about capabilities

These principles aren't just words—they're actions that demonstrate your beliefs and create consistent results. When what people see and hear from you aligns with these values, you achieve a level of authenticity that resonates deeply with potential clients.

Let me get more into this, Integrity isn't just about doing the right thing—it's about having the courage to say "no" when you know you can't deliver what the client needs. I've watched countless sales professionals nod their heads and say "yes" to everything, promising capabilities they don't have or results they can't guarantee, all to close the deal. This short-term thinking might fill your pipeline today, but it destroys trust and burns bridges tomorrow.

For example, I recently turned down a potential client because I knew their needs would be better served by a different type of business development approach than what I offer. While it meant passing on immediate revenue, it maintained my integrity and led to a referral relationship that has produced even more valuable opportunities. I have turned down many opportunities simply because I knew it was not going to serve the client's needs and referred out to someone who could help them. This actually solidified my capabilities to them and honesty that I truly want to help them beyond what I could provide.

Innovation: Beyond Quick Fixes

True innovation isn't about forcing your standard solution to fit every problem. It's about having the wisdom and creativity to look at challenges from different angles. Too often, sales professionals try to hammer square pegs into round holes because they're focused on making quota rather than solving real problems. This one-dimensional approach might work for a single transaction, but it never builds lasting relationships.

Honesty: The Courage to Be Clear

Being honest about your capabilities isn't just about listing what you can do—it's about being upfront about what you can't do. In my experience, clients respect and appreciate clear boundaries. When you're transparent about your limitations and realistic about outcomes, you build the kind of trust that leads to long-term partnerships rather than one-off deals.

These principles aren't just nice words to put on your website—they're actions that should guide every client interaction. When what people see and hear from you consistently aligns with these values, you achieve a level of authenticity that resonates deeply with potential clients and creates lasting relationships rather than just transactions.

Moving From Helper to Solution Provider: A New Way to Communicate Value

Let's transform how we communicate our value to potential clients. Instead of leading with "I help people with..." which can sound vague and passive, let's focus on the transformative results we deliver. Think of it as painting a before-and-after picture with your words.

The Power of Visual Transformation

One of my favorite exercises with clients is surprisingly simple but incredibly powerful: I ask them to draw two pictures. The first shows their client when they first seek help - often depicting stress, confusion, or overwhelm. The second shows their client after working together - typically showing confidence, success, and peace of mind. This visual exercise brings clarity to the true value you provide and helps craft a more compelling message.

Here's how to transform your message:

Instead of: "I help people organize their finances" Say: "People come to me feeling overwhelmed by financial chaos and leave with clear systems and confidence about their future"

Instead of: "I help businesses improve their operations" Say: "Business owners come to me working 80-hour weeks and leave with streamlined systems that let them take vacations while their business grows"

This approach does two powerful things:

1. It acknowledges where your clients are starting (their pain point)

2. It paints a vivid picture of their transformation (their desired outcome)

Real-World Examples of Transformation Messages

For a **Wellness Coach**: Before: "I help people get healthy" After: "People come to me exhausted and stressed, and discover how to create sustainable energy that lasts all day"

For a **Financial Advisor**: Before: "I help people plan for retirement" After: "People come to me worried about their financial future and leave knowing exactly how they'll fund their dream retirement"

For a **Business Consultant**: Before: "I help businesses grow" After: "Business owners come to me stuck at six figures and leave with scalable systems that take them to seven"

The key is to be specific about both the starting point and the transformation. When you clearly articulate this journey, potential clients can see themselves in your story and understand exactly how working with you will change their situation.

Try this exercise yourself:

1. Draw your typical client when they first come to you
2. Draw them after your work together is complete
3. List the specific changes you see
4. Craft your message around this transformation

Remember, people don't buy services - they buy transformations. When you can clearly communicate the journey from pain to solution, you make it easier for potential clients to say "yes" to working with you.

UNDERSTANDING YOUR
IDEAL CLIENT

Let's bring your ideal client to life - literally!

First, draw their expression:
Are they smiling, stressed, confused?
What's their immediate pain point?

Around their head, draw thought bubbles
with:
Their biggest worries
What keeps them up at night
What they're desperately wanting

Around them, add labels for:
Their job title/role
Age range
Key demographics
Where you'd find them

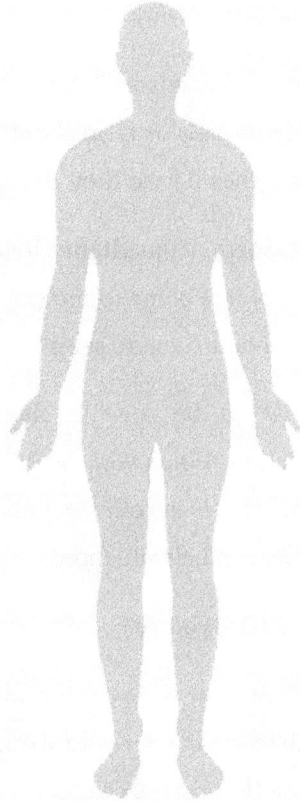

UNDERSTANDING YOUR IDEAL CLIENT

THE TRANSFORMATION SKETCH

Now draw them AFTER working with you:

- How has their expression changed?
- What new thought bubbles appear?
- What have they let go of?
- What new things are they holding?

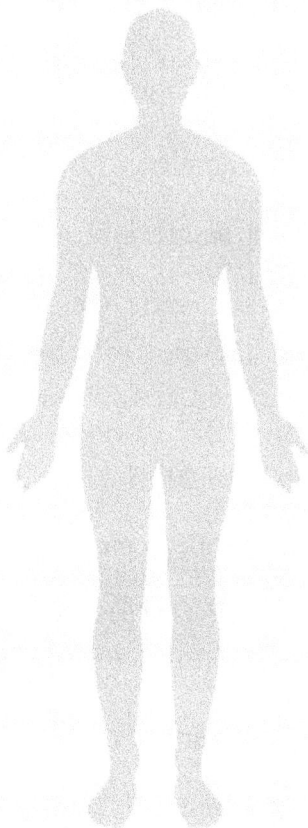

The Shift: From Features to Feelings

Think of this as your field guide to industry-specific networking. I'm about to share real examples, proven strategies, and practical approaches tailored to different professional backgrounds. Whether you're in financial services, healthcare, real estate, or any other field, you're about to see exactly how successful professionals in your industry build meaningful connections that drive results. I'm going to offer more examples in hopes this will resonate in your industry.

Financial Services

Before: "I help businesses secure funding"

After: "Business owners come to me stressed about cash flow and growth limitations, and leave with the capital and confidence to seize every opportunity that comes their way"

Business Lending

Instead of: "We offer competitive interest rates and flexible terms"

Say: "Imagine sleeping peacefully at night knowing you have the capital to seize every growth opportunity that comes your way"

Business Coaching

Before: "I help businesses scale"

After: "Entrepreneurs come to me working 80-hour weeks and drowning in operations, and leave with systems that let them focus on growth while their team handles the day-to-day"

Employee Benefits

Before: "I help companies with benefits packages"

After: "Companies come to me losing top talent and struggling with retention, and leave with a benefits strategy that makes them the employer everyone wants to work for"

Non-Profit Leadership

Before: "I help raise funds for community programs"

After: "Donors come to me wanting to make a difference but unsure how, and leave seeing exactly how their contribution transforms lives in our community"

Alternative Healing

Before: "I help people with energy alignment"

After: "People come to me feeling drained and disconnected, and discover how to maintain their inner peace even during life's biggest challenges"

Commercial Banking

Before: "I help businesses with banking solutions"

After: "Business owners come to me juggling multiple accounts and worried about cash flow, and leave with streamlined operations and clear visibility into their financial future"

Mortgage Advising

Before: "I help people secure home loans"

After: "First-time buyers come to me anxious about the home-buying process, and leave confidently holding the keys to their dream home with a payment plan that fits their lifestyle"

Business Banking

Before: "I'm a business banker offering competitive rates and treasury management solutions."

After: Business owners come to me when they're ready to stop worrying about day-to-day cash flow and start focusing on growth opportunities. They leave knowing they have a strategic financial partner who understands their business goals, not just their banking needs."

Estate Planning Attorney

Before: "I help families plan their estates"

After: "People come to me worried about their family's future security, and leave knowing their legacy will protect and provide for generations to come"

The key in each transformation is moving from technical features to emotional outcomes. People don't buy what you do—they buy how it will make them feel and how it will transform their lives. When you speak to these deeper emotional needs, you create connections that resonate on a human level rather than just a business one.

Creating Your Authentic Sales Approach

To develop your own authentic sales message:

1. Write down your three most common customer problems.
2. For each problem, identify the emotional impact.
3. Craft your message around solving that emotional pain.
4. Practice telling stories about transformations, not transactions.

Remember: Features explain, but feelings sell. People make decisions with their hearts and justify them with their heads.

The Three Breakthrough Truths

Success comes when we embrace these fundamental principles:

1. Selling with soul isn't about pushing—it's about allowing. When you truly believe in your offering, selling becomes an act of service.
2. Authenticity is your superpower. Your relatability and trustworthiness come from being genuine.
3. Focus on connection before conversion. Every meaningful sale starts with a human connection.

Your expertise matters—it's why you can deliver amazing results. But it's not why people buy. They buy because you understand their dreams, their fears, and their desires. Stop pitching your process, and start promising their perfect outcome. That's how you transform from being one-dimensional in sales to creating genuine connections that convert.

The Continuous Journey of Connection

Key Takeaways from Our Journey Together

As we conclude our exploration of authentic networking and relationship building, let's reflect on the essential lessons from each chapter that will guide your continued growth:

Chapter 1: Beyond the Business Card Shuffle

- Authentic connections begin with genuine curiosity and active listening
- Strong foundations require careful groundwork and intentional relationship building
- The most valuable professional relationships often start with personal connection
- Quality of interaction matters more than quantity of contacts
- Trust building is a gradual process that requires consistent, authentic behavior

Chapter 2: Developing a Magnetic Presence

- Authentic confidence comes from alignment between internal beliefs and external presentation
- Your presence begins before you enter a room—it starts with how you feel about yourself
- Body language and non-verbal communication speak louder than words
- Professional polish should enhance, not hide, your authentic self

- Your personal brand is the sum of every interaction, not just your curated image

Chapter 3: Streamline Your Networking Approach

- Strategic networking requires clear objectives and thoughtful preparation
- Different types of connections require different approaches and time investments
- Social media should complement, not replace, in-person relationship building
- Follow-up is where the real relationship building begins
- Energy management is crucial for sustainable networking success

Chapter 4: Mastering the Value Exchange

- True value extends far beyond services or products offered
- The best connections create unexpected opportunities for all involved
- Value creation is about transformation, not transaction
- Genuine support and strategic introductions build lasting relationships
- The compound effect of consistent value-adding creates exponential returns

Chapter 5: Ditch the Pitch

- People buy transformations, not features or services
- Authentic selling comes from understanding and addressing emotional needs
- Your story should focus on the journey from pain to solution
- Integrity, innovation, and honesty form the foundation of lasting business relationships

- The most powerful sales approach is one that aligns with your authentic self

Moving Forward: Your Continuous Journey

The stories we've shared—of Michele, Michael, Kim, and countless others—demonstrate that the most extraordinary opportunities often emerge from the most unexpected places. Embracing the unknown, staying open to new perspectives, and maintaining an authentic curiosity about others' journeys are the true cornerstones of professional success.

Remember that these principles are not meant to be mastered and forgotten, but rather integrated into your daily professional life. Each interaction is an opportunity to:

- Practice authentic connection
- Create meaningful value
- Build lasting relationships
- Transform lives through genuine support
- Grow your own professional presence

The most powerful aspect of authentic networking is that it creates a positive cycle: as you help others succeed, you naturally attract more opportunities to make an impact. Your network becomes not just a professional asset, but a community of mutual support and growth.

Your Next Steps

1. Choose one key takeaway from each chapter to implement immediately
2. Set specific goals for relationship building in your professional community
3. Create a system for consistent follow-up and value creation

4. Regularly assess and adjust your networking approach
5. Stay committed to authentic connection over quick transactions

Remember, your most meaningful professional relationships may start with a simple conversation, grow through consistent nurturing, and blossom into unexpected opportunities. Stay open to possibilities, remain genuine in your interactions, and trust that authentic networking will continue to transform both your professional journey and the lives of those you connect with.

Your network is not just a collection of contacts—it's a living ecosystem of relationships, opportunities, and potential. Nurture it with authenticity, grow it with intention, and watch as it transforms not just your career, but your entire professional journey.

Remember that little girl who once coordinated neighborhood puppet shows and managed Avon orders with remarkable efficiency? She understood something profound about connection long before she knew what networking meant. From organizing kids to create magical performances to helping her mother build a business, the seeds of relationship-building were always there.

You may not consider yourself a natural connector or networker—and that's okay. This book is your comprehensive toolkit, filled with real-life experiences, practical strategies, and actionable insights that will transform how you approach professional relationships. Whether you're an introvert, an extrovert, or somewhere in between, these principles will empower you to build meaningful connections that drive your business forward.

Strategic connections are not just professional courtesies—they are economic engines. A single meaningful introduction can:

- Generate immediate revenue opportunities
- Create long-term collaborative partnerships

- Reduce customer acquisition costs
- Open doors to markets previously unavailable

We are all in business with a common goal: growth. In today's interconnected world, making meaningful connections isn't just a skill— it's a vital lifeline for any professional seeking to expand their horizons, create opportunities, and drive success. Your network is the bridge between where you are and where you want to be.

The end of this book is not the end of your networking journey—it's your launching pad. I challenge you to take immediate action:

Within the next 7 days:

- Identify three connections in your network who could benefit from a meaningful introduction
- Schedule one intentional networking conversation
- Review and update your personal value proposition
- Commit to one authentic, value-adding action for someone in your professional community

Your network is not just a collection of contacts—it's a living ecosystem of relationships, opportunities, and potential. By implementing the strategies in this book, you're not just improving your professional connections; you're becoming a catalyst for collective growth.

Start now. Reach out to that contact you've been meaning to connect with. Make that introduction. Share that insight. Your most transformative professional relationship might be just one genuine conversation away.

The journey of authentic networking is continuous. Your most powerful professional asset is your capacity to see potential in others and create environments where that potential can flourish. Are you ready to transform your network—and yourself?

Ready to Transform Your Professional Relationships?

Stop wasting time on networking that doesn't work. In "Explosive Connections: Building Business Through Strategic Relationships," you'll discover the proven strategies that have helped thousands of professionals in my sales training workshops build meaningful connections that drive real business results.

Get your copy today and start:

- Identifying your ideal connections faster
- Developing a magnetic professional presence
- Creating conversations that convert
- Building a network that generates consistent opportunities

Order now and transform your approach to professional relationships from the ground up.

Connect with Me

Ready to take your networking to the next level? Visit me at **justjanelle.com** to learn more about my sales training workshops, business development consulting, and additional resources for building powerful professional relationships.

Let's connect and start building the relationships that will transform your business success.

www.ingramcontent.com/pod-product-compliance
Lightning Source LLC
Chambersburg PA
CBHW071711210326
41597CB00017B/2442